SCIENTISTS AND THEIR DISCOVERIES

ALEXANDER FLEMING

SCIENTISTS AND THEIR DISCOVERIES

ALBERT EINSTEIN

ALEXANDER FLEMING

ALFRED NOBEL

BENJAMIN FRANKLIN

CHARLES DARWIN

GALILEO

GREGOR MENDEL

ISAAC NEWTON

LEONARDO DA VINCI

LOUIS PASTEUR

THOMAS EDISON

SCIENTISTS AND THEIR DISCOVERIES

ALEXANDER FLEMING

BRADLEY SNEDDON

MASON CREST

Mason Crest
450 Parkway Drive, Suite D
Broomall, Pennsylvania 19008
(866) MCP-BOOK (toll-free)
www.masoncrest.com

Printed and bound in the United States of America.

CPSIA Compliance Information: Batch #SG2018.
For further information, contact Mason Crest at 1-866-MCP-Book.

First printing
9 8 7 6 5 4 3 2 1

Library of Congress Cataloging-in-Publication Data

ISBN: 978-1-4222-4025-0 (hc)
ISBN: 978-1-4222-7757-7 (ebook)

Scientists and their Discoveries series ISBN: 978-1-4222-4023-6

Developed and Produced by National Highlights Inc.
Interior and cover design: Yolanda Van Cooten
Production: Michelle Luke

QR CODES AND LINKS TO THIRD-PARTY CONTENT
You may gain access to certain third-party content ("Third-Party Sites") by scanning and using the QR Codes that appear in this publication (the "QR Codes"). We do not operate or control in any respect any information, products, or services on such Third-Party Sites linked to by us via the QR Codes included in this publication, and we assume no responsibility for any materials you may access using the QR Codes. Your use of the QR Codes may be subject to terms, limitations, or restrictions set forth in the applicable terms of use or otherwise established by the owners of the Third-Party Sites. Our linking to such Third-Party Sites via the QR Codes does not imply an endorsement or sponsorship of such Third-Party Sites or the information, products, or services offered on or through the Third-Party Sites, nor does it imply an endorsement or sponsorship of this publication by the owners of such Third-Party Sites.

Publisher's Note: Websites listed in this book were active at the time of publication. The publisher is not responsible for websites that have changed their address or discontinued operation since the date of publication. The publisher reviews and updates the websites each time the book is reprinted.

CONTENTS

CHAPTER 1   The Strange Route to St. Mary's 7

CHAPTER 2   Working in Bacteriology 19

CHAPTER 3   War and Aftermath 33

CHAPTER 4   The Discovery of Penicillin 47

CHAPTER 5   The Period of Failure and Neglect 59

CHAPTER 6   Penicillin and the Second World War 71

Chronology 84

Further Reading 88

Internet Resources 89

Series Glossary of Key Terms 90

Index 93

About the Author 96

KEY ICONS TO LOOK FOR:

Words to understand: These words with their easy-to-understand definitions will increase the reader's understanding of the text while building vocabulary skills.

Sidebars: This boxed material within the main text allows readers to build knowledge, gain insights, explore possibilities, and broaden their perspectives by weaving together additional information to provide realistic and holistic perspectives.

Educational videos: Readers can view videos by scanning our QR codes, providing them with additional educational content to supplement the text. Examples include news coverage, moments in history, speeches, iconic sports moments, and much more!

Text-dependent questions: These questions send the reader back to the text for more careful attention to the evidence presented there.

Research projects: Readers are pointed toward areas of further inquiry connected to each chapter. Suggestions are provided for projects that encourage deeper research and analysis.

Series glossary of key terms: This back-of-the-book glossary contains terminology used throughout the series. Words found here increase the reader's ability to read and comprehend higher-level books and articles in this field.

The rolling hills of Ayrshire, a county in southwestern Scotland. Alexander Fleming grew up on a farm not far from this area.

WORDS TO UNDERSTAND

honours—in the British educational system, students who earn undergraduate degrees with the highest grades or performance are awarded a "degree with honours."

kirk—a Scottish word meaning "church," particularly one belonging to the Church of Scotland, a Protestant Christian denomination known in the United States as the Presbyterian Church.

public school—in the United Kingdom, this is the term for a private, tuition-charging school that provided secondary education. In Fleming's time, public school students were young men whose families were members of Britain's upper or upper-middle classes.

CHAPTER 1

The Strange Route to St. Mary's

Alexander Fleming was born in southwestern Scotland in 1881, on a lonely farm called Lochfield in Ayrshire, bordering on Renfrewshire and Lanarkshire. His father, a hill farmer, had married twice, having four children by each marriage. Alec, as his family and friends called him, was the second youngest of the eight Fleming children.

When they were not at school, Alec would explore the hills and the moorland with his brothers and sister. Hunting—without guns—and fishing developed his powers of observation. From a very early age, Alec had a love of sport that was to last throughout his life, and which was to play a big part in determining his career.

Life at the farm was secluded—their nearest neighbors were a mile away. Only at the village school at Loudoun Moor, or at the **kirk**, would Alec have met anyone outside his own family, and the school had one class of only twelve or fifteen children with one teacher.

At the age of ten, Alec moved on to the school at Darvel, the nearest town. He would make the four-mile walk in all weathers. He worked well there and at the age of twelve went to the academy at Kilmarnock for about eighteen months.

Alec's father had died when he and his brothers were still very young and they had few memories of him. His mother, Grace, was left to run the farm with the help of the eldest son, Hugh. The Flemings were not a poor family, but knowing that the farm could not support more than one of them, the rest of the family now had to earn their living away from home.

Two of Alec's older brothers, Tom and John, were already in London by the time he had finished at Kilmarnock. Originally intending to be a family doctor, Tom had decided to specialize in diseases of the eye, becoming an "oculist," and John was learning to become an optician. Alec, now fourteen years old, traveled south to stay with them in 1897. He was followed to London six months later by Robert, his younger brother.

For the next two years, Alec Fleming attended lectures at the Polytechnic School on Regent Street in London. At the end of this time, he found a job as a clerk in

Loudoun Hill, a few miles from the Fleming farm at Lochfield, was a popular climbing spot for active young men like Alexander. In the fourteenth century, it was the site of major battles against English forces during the Scottish War for Independence.

a shipping office. Fleming did not enjoy the work, but he had little choice—he needed the money.

In 1900, when the Boer War became serious, John, Alec, and later Robert joined the Territorial Army, which was formed to defend the United Kingdom territories so that the British Army could be sent to South Africa. The Fleming brothers enlisted in a Territorial Army unit called the London Scottish, a regiment largely composed of men of Scottish descent. Most of the men never saw any action. However, the London Scottish gave Alec a great opportunity to indulge in his love for sports. All three brothers played for the regiment's water polo team, and Alec turned out to be quite a good shot, also. To everyone's surprise, H Company—traditionally the most awkward bunch in the regiment—carried off the shooting trophy, largely due to the marksmanship of Alexander Fleming.

Medical School

Fleming would, perhaps, have remained in the business world all of his life, but his Uncle John, a bachelor, had died in 1901, leaving him just enough money to take up his brother John's suggestion that he should go to college and study medicine. Alec Fleming applied for a University of London scholarship in natural sciences, and won in July 1901. He earned the highest scores of all candidates in the United Kingdom.

Fleming intended to be a surgeon, perhaps specializing in eye diseases like his brother. There were twelve medical schools in London, but he chose to attend St. Mary's Hospital in the Paddington neighborhood. Fleming later said that he chose St. Mary's because he had played water polo against the school's team while with the London Scottish regiment, and had liked them. This turned out to be a fortunate decision.

Because of the time Fleming had spent as a clerk, he was a little older than most of the others in his school class, but he never regretted that fact. "I gained much general knowledge," he later said, "and when I went to medical school I had a great advantage over my fellow students, who were straight from school and never got away from their books into the school of life."

Fleming was a brilliant student, earning most of the awards in his class. When he took his final University of London examinations, he got **honours** in five subjects and was awarded the university gold medal. Still intending to be a surgeon, he also took the fellowship examination for the Royal College of Surgeons.

Fleming's outstanding success in examinations might give the impression that he worked very hard and studied all of the time, but this was not the case. He had a very good memory and he found the work interesting and easy. He managed to find plenty of time for his sports—shooting and swimming.

For a second time, athletics would play a vital role in determining the course that Fleming's career would take. A young doctor in the bacteriology department named John Freeman was on the lookout for people who could strengthen the St. Mary's shooting team. He knew that Fleming was a good shot and badly wanted him to stay at the hospital. Unfortunately, there was only one surgical vacancy at St. Mary's, and despite his school accomplishments, Fleming was not sure to get the spot. After a good deal of persuasion, Freeman managed to win Fleming over to the idea that he should work in the bacteriology department. All that Freeman now had to do was to convince his "chief," Sir Almroth Wright, to make the invitation.

This was not difficult, as it turned out. Freeman did not try to hide his reasons for wanting Fleming. He pointed out quite bluntly that Fleming was good with his hands, worked well, and had a scientific mind—but most important of all, he was a good shot and would be just the man for his precious shooting team. Wright was amused, and so Fleming was welcomed aboard.

Opposite page: Wounded soldiers are removed from the battlefield in this illustration made during the Boer War. Fleming joined a regiment in London that was part of the Territorial Army, a reserve force that would remain to defend England, allowing regiments of the regular army to be sent to South Africa.

Life at St. Mary's

The Bacteriology Department at St. Mary's was a strange place for Fleming. He seemed to be the complete opposite of everyone else there. Fleming was state-educated—a scholarship boy from a polytechnic school. He was small, very quiet and reserved, and spoke with a broad Scottish accent. He found himself surrounded by ex-army men, mostly officers and mainly from the older universities and **public schools**. They were tall men—several more than six feet tall. They called Wright, who was the most senior officer among them, "the Old Man," in the same way that a ship's crew would refer to their captain. Fleming had one thing in common with all these others. He adored the Old Man and wanted only to please him.

Fleming was one of the second generation of bacteriologists in Britain. Whereas the pioneers of a science have to find their way entirely alone, those who follow are taught at least some of the subject. The directions for further investigation are often set by the teacher, at least to start with, and Fleming and the other students who joined Wright's department were put to work on the things that interested the Old Man.

Today, medical research work is paid for by large pharmaceutical companies, often supplemented by grants from government health services. But in the first half of the twentieth century, research was often conducted by medical professionals as a hobby, and was paid for out of their other earnings or from private funds.

Wright, like most senior workers in the department, had a private medical practice. He persuaded his patients to donate money so that he could conduct research at the hospital. Wright and his team of students would devote their evenings to their research, after a full day's work in the hospital.

Opposite page: The entrance to St. Mary's Hospital on Praed Street in Paddington, London, where Alexander Fleming received his medical training.

John Freeman (1877–1962) recruited Fleming to take a post in the bacteriology department at St. Mary's—mainly so he could contribute to the shooting team. The two men would be colleagues for many years, with each expecting to eventually succeed Almroth Wright as head of the bacteriology department.

At four o'clock there was tea in the library, a very small room at the top of a turret staircase. A small table, a few kitchen chairs, and a couch was all that there was in the way of furniture. A kettle on a small stove provided boiling water, and tea was served in an odd collection of cups and mugs. There was enough food to keep the team going until ten o'clock, when there was a second tea break before they went home. Some would stay even later if their work was interesting or had to be completed that night.

The main purpose of the four o'clock meetings was to talk about work. The results of the previous day's experiments would be reported, and they would all discuss them. After this Wright would talk about any new ideas he had. Finally, they would plan the night's work.

The late-night meetings were similar, but they were often attended by visitors who would come there to talk with Wright. These included his old friend George Bernard Shaw, the famous playwright; statesmen like Lord Balfour; and industrialists like Arthur Guinness.

Almroth Edward Wright (1861–1947), head of the Inoculation Department, St. Mary's Hospital.

For a short film on modern lab workers at St. Mary's Hospital, scan here:

Fleming attended these meetings and learned from them, but they were not the sort of occasion that really suited him. He was for the most part silent and made no conversation. If he had to report, he did so in the shortest possible way. His value was in the laboratory, not in the library.

Because of this way of organizing things, it was almost impossible to tell who was responsible for the ideas that emerged. In this type of "round table" discussion, the idea that comes out at the end and on which an experiment is based might be so different from the original suggestion that no one person can claim—or deserves—the credit.

Thus for the first part of his career, Fleming was forced to work as part of a team. All his work in those days was the result of the efforts of the group as a whole. It was to be twenty years before he published anything that could be said to be entirely his own.

TEXT-DEPENDENT QUESTIONS

1. Where was Alexander Fleming born?
2. Why did Fleming choose to study at St. Mary's?
3. Who was the "Old Man?"

RESEARCH PROJECT

Some of history's most important scientists were born and educated in Scotland. In addition to Alexander Fleming, they include Alexander Graham Bell, Joseph Black, Robert Brown, James Hutton, Joseph Lister, James Clerk Maxwell, and James Watt. Using the internet or your school library, find out more about a Scottish scientist. Write a two-page report and share it with your class.

$E = mgh$ $p = mv$ $E = mc^2$ mv^2 $a = F/m$

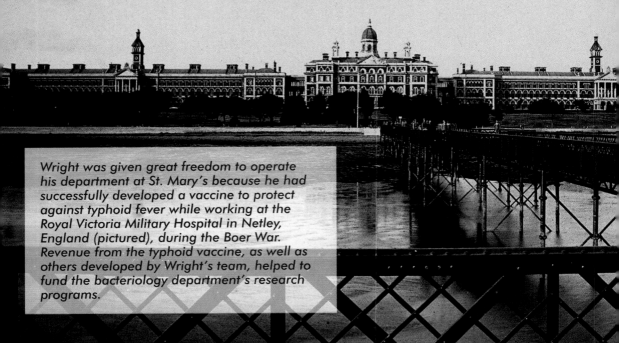

Wright was given great freedom to operate his department at St. Mary's because he had successfully developed a vaccine to protect against typhoid fever while working at the Royal Victoria Military Hospital in Netley, England (pictured), during the Boer War. Revenue from the typhoid vaccine, as well as others developed by Wright's team, helped to fund the bacteriology department's research programs.

 ## WORDS TO UNDERSTAND

allergist—a scientist that studies allergies, which are physical reactions to certain substances that a patient's body rejects, such as certain foods, grass pollen, or animal dander.

attenuate—to make a culture of germs weaker, or harmless, without actually killing them.

bacillus—a rod-shaped organism. The word is used usually for special groups such as typhoid.

bacteriology—a branch of microbiology that deals with the identification, study, and cultivation of bacteria, for use in medicine and other areas.

immunology—the study of the defenses of the body.

syphilis—the most serious venereal disease, caught from an infected person by very close contact.

vaccine—a preparation made from cultures of organisms that are safe to inject into people to create immunity.

CHAPTER 2

Working in Bacteriology

When Fleming joined the **bacteriology** department research team headed by Almroth Wright, it included four scientists who would go on to distinguished careers: Stewart Ranken Douglas, Bernard Spilsbury, John Freeman, and Leonard Noon. Douglas had been a captain in the British Army's medical service, but left the service in 1901 to work with Wright. Spilsbury worked in Wright's department for several years, then left to work as a pathologist, using science in the detection of crime.

Freeman was tall, athletic, and handsome. During the Boer War (1899–1902), he had interrupted his studies at Oxford to join the Territorial Army. A most charming man—his patients adored him—he was always full of ideas, but was upset whenever they were opposed. "He blew in, blew up and blew out," a colleague once said of him when he was in one of these moods. He and Leonard Noon were among the first full-time **allergists** in the world. They pioneered the successful treatment of hay fever and many types of asthma, particularly those due to animals such as household dogs and cats, and feathers in bedding.

Fleming joined the team in 1906, followed soon after by Leonard Colebrook. Colebrook was very different from Fleming. The son of a parson, he had intended to become a medical missionary but Wright had persuaded him to work in the laboratory instead. He was greatly devoted to his work.

SIR ALMROTH WRIGHT

Almroth Wright, the Old Man of the bacteriology department, would work with Alec Fleming for nearly fifty years.

Almroth Edward Wright was the son of an Irish clergyman. His mother was Swedish. Wright went to school in various towns throughout Europe and attended college in Ireland.

In 1892 he became a professor in the British Army, teaching the men in the Royal Army Medical Corps to study the diseases that attacked British troops overseas, especially in hot countries. The work that they did together helped to pinpoint the causes of a great many tropical illnesses.

Typhoid fever, a frightening and often fatal disease, got special attention from Wright. In 1896 he announced that he had made a vaccine that would prevent it, and in 1899, when the Boer War broke out, he tried to persuade the War Office to use his vaccine on the troops. The War Office was so unhelpful, and used his vaccine so badly, that in 1902 Wright left the army in disgust and went to St. Mary's Hospital as Professor of Pathology. This was about the same time that Fleming started there as a medical student.

Many of the brightest students went to Wright's department. Some stayed for only a year or two and then went on to follow some other line of work. Others remained in the laboratories for the rest of their lives. Those lives, however, might well be short, for nothing was then known of the risks that laboratory workers ran. Two members of Wright's team, Noon and John Herbert Wells, were to die from diseases caught from their work. Nurses and medical students in those days were also constantly at risk, particularly from tuberculosis.

Colebrook later moved to Queen Charlotte's Hospital, where he concentrated on deadly childbed fever. Through his efforts many lives were saved and much pain and discomfort avoided. Colebrook's work in this field of medicine was as great as Joseph Lister's on antisepsis— the use of chemicals to kill germs—was to surgery.

Freeman, Fleming, and Colebrook were each in their own way very valuable men to Wright. Freeman was his devoted admirer and a great talker—always starting off ideas. Colebrook was steady, reliable, and his lifelong friend. Fleming brought skill to the invention of new methods and could carry out experiments so carefully that he outdid everyone else in accuracy. Wright called them his "sons in science," and encouraged a close family feel in his department at St. Mary's.

Leonard Noon (1878–1913) was close friends with John Freeman. In 1911, they made groundbreaking discoveries related to allergies, specifically hay fever.

Work of a Bacteriologist

What exactly was the work that these men were doing? Very broadly speaking, bacteriologists throughout the world were trying to find out how the body learns to destroy disease organisms that invade it, and how doctors could help the body tackle this job more effectively. Wright's experience in hot countries, particularly

Antonie van Leeuwenhoek (1632–1723) observed tiny living things, including bacteria, for the first time through a microscope during the seventeenth century.

Egypt and India, led him to concentrate on **vaccines** that would prevent illness. To see how his work fits in to the way medical knowledge was developing, we must go back, briefly, to the discovery of bacteria in 1683.

Antonie van Leeuwenhoek was one of the first users of the microscope. In 1683, he found that rainwater, after contact with city air, contained "little animals" 10,000 times smaller than the water fleas that he could see with his naked eye. He also observed material scraped from inside of his own mouth under the microscope, and drew pictures of the tiny creatures that he saw. Leeuwenhoek had discovered the tiny organisms that would later be called "germs" or "microbes." However, he did not recognize any connection between these organisms and disease. Discovery of bacteria and other tiny animals was one thing; proving that they cause disease was quite another.

The first man to show that one of these minute germs does cause illness was an Italian, Agostino Bassi. He spent twenty years studying the disease *muscardine* in silkworms, and showed that it is due to a tiny fungus. Thirty years later, in 1866, the Frenchman Louis Pasteur, also working on sickness in silkworms, showed that the disease *pébrine* was caused by a living organism—and one that actually lived, grew, and bred inside the silkworm itself!

The first disease affecting humans that Pasteur tackled successfully was anthrax. This disease normally attacks sheep and cattle, but sometimes it spreads to people, causing serious health problems. The anthrax microbe, called a **bacillus** because of its rod-like shape, was discovered in 1849 in the blood of cattle that had anthrax by a German scientist, Franz Aloys Pollender. In 1868, a Frenchman, Casimir Joseph Davaine, showed that these tiny bacilli were present in every case of anthrax that he studied. That, however, was not enough to prove that they caused the disease. Proof came in 1877, when Pasteur managed to produce pure cultures of these bacilli. When he injected them into test animals in the laboratory, they produced anthrax just as surely as an injection of infected blood would. This proved beyond doubt that, in the case of anthrax at least, the germ theory was right. The biggest step was still to come.

In 1880, Pasteur was studying the bacilli of another disease, fowl cholera. He discovered that this germ could be weakened, or **attenuated**, by growing

Louis Pasteur (1822–95) was a French microbiologist whose work proved the germ theory of disease. Pasteur also pioneered immunization as a defense against diseases.

the germ in a certain way. More importantly, when he injected chickens with an attenuated culture of fowl cholera, they did not develop the disease—even after being subsequently injected with the full-strengh germ.

Pasteur then applied this lesson to what he knew about anthrax. In May of 1881, in a much-publicized test, he injected fifty sheep with the anthrax bacilli. Twenty-five of the sheep had previously been injected with an attenuated strain of the bacilli, so that they could develop an immunity. The other twenty-five sheep were unprotected. All of the previously vaccinated sheep survived the trial, while all the unvaccinated sheep contracted anthrax and were dead in less than a week.

Pasteur's achievements changed the face of modern medicine. Before Pasteur, most doctors refused to admit the existence of germs at all—in spite of the mounting evidence to the contrary. But, backed up by followers and pioneers such as Joseph Lister in Scotland and Robert Koch in Germany, Pasteur succeeded in breaking down the opposition to this new approach to disease. His spectacular results in immunization against anthrax, and later against rabies, forced even the rather conservative medical profession to accept his ideas.

Two important questions now needed answers. The first was: How, exactly, does the body destroy the germs that invade it? The second was: How does the body learn to kill germs?

Scan here for a short video on the origin of vaccines:

Joseph Lister (1827–1912) was one of Pasteur's foremost supporters in trying to get the germ theory of disease accepted. He was an English surgeon and the founder of antiseptic surgery.

It was evident that the body does learn. One of Pasteur's students was a Russian named Elie Metchnikoff. Working in Italy in the early 1880s, Metchnikoff discovered that the white cells of the blood surround and destroy certain invading bacteria. However, Metchnikoff was unable to explain how the white blood cells did this. Numerous studies in the late nineteenth century had shown that after a person suffered from an illness, the white blood cells would kill the germs that caused that illness much more effectively than it had previously. This is why a person only suffers from certain diseases, such as measles, mumps, and chicken pox, only once.

German bacteriologist Robert Koch (1843–1910) built on Pasteur's work in microbiology, showing how bacteria caused certain diseases. Koch developed a way of classifying bacteria and of proving whether particular bacteria were the causes of a sickness or just innocent bystanders.

Almroth Wright was fascinated by the question of how the body develops immunity to diseases. He believed it might be possible to treat illnesses that had already been contracted, by giving a vaccine in just the right dose that would help the white blood cells do better than they were already doing. In other words, he believed in vaccinations that would help cure diseases, as well as vaccinations that would prevent people from contracting them in the first place. It was this curative aspect of vaccines on which Wright's department concentrated.

Fighting Disease

In those days there were, in theory, three approaches to the treatment of patients who already had a disease. The first was by methods of **immunology**. In these methods the body is stimulated to produce its own, natural defenses against bacteria. This was the method favored by Wright in his research. Second, there was the use of antiseptics—chemicals that kill any form of living cell. Although antiseptics are useful for preventing disease by killing harmful bacteria before they can cause an infection, they are not as useful once a patient has contracted an infection. Third was a relatively new idea: that there might be substances, called **chemotherapeutic agents**, that somehow singled out certain germs—living cells within the body, such as harmful bacteria—and killed them without causing harm to other body cells.

Mercury and quinine were among the few substances that people considered chemotherapeutic agents in the early twentieth century. Mercury, a heavy metal that is highly toxic to humans, had been used since at least 1493 to treat **syphilis**, a venereal disease. However, by Fleming's time most doctors recognized that mercury treatments could only limit the symptoms, but could not cure this disease. Quinine, which is derived from the bark of the Cinchona tree in South America, was more effective. It was developed in the 1820s and used to treat malaria. Previously, other bark extracts had been used to treat malaria since at least the 1630s.

Most bacteriologists at that time had received very little in the way of chemical training. Almroth Wright had grave doubts about the usefulness of chemotherapeutic agents. There was, however, one bacteriologist working at this time who was also an outstanding chemist. He was a German named Paul Ehrlich.

Ehrlich was looking for a drug that could be used to cure syphilis. This venereal disease was quite common and was greatly feared because it was incurable and could be passed on to children. In 1905, the organism that caused syphilis, a bacteria called *Treponema pallidum*, was identified by Fritz Schaudinn and Erich Hoffmann.

In studying *Treponema pallidum* under a microscope, Ehrlich used a range of colored chemical dyes to stain the bacteria. This was done to make it easier to see under a microscope, compared to the healthy tissue. Ehrlich had the idea that if these dyes could be made poisonous to the bacteria that they found and stained, then doctors might have something like a "magic bullet" that could be used to attack diseases while leaving healthy tissue alone. The problem was finding a way to load the dye with poison and still keep it aimed at its special target. After years of work on a series of dyes called "anilines," to which

Elie Metchnikoff (1845–1916) was a Russian biologist. He showed that the white cells of the blood "eat" certain invading bacteria.

Ehrlich tried to attach such poisonous substances as arsenic and antimony, he at last came up with a success. It was number 606 in his series of tests, and thus became known simply as "606."

Some of this new substance was sent to Wright's institute for testing. The testing of this new substance, however, was left to Fleming. After all, it was a chemical. Wright was only interested in immunity. He thought of 606 more as a curiosity than anything else.

There were quite difficult surgical problems involved in giving the drug to patients. Because so little of it would dissolve in water, it had to be made up in huge volumes. It also had to be prepared in sterile conditions and given immediately by injection into a vein. Although getting blood out of a vein had

Paul Ehrlich (1854–1915), a German scientist and one of the pioneers of bacteriology, at work in his laboratory. He developed the drug salversan (606), some of which he sent to Wright's Institute to test on patients suffering from syphilis. Fleming's successful tests showed that salversan was one of the first modern chemotherapeutic agents. In 1908 Ehrlich shared with Metchnikoff the Nobel Prize for Medicine.

been done for hundreds of years, putting anything into one with any success was a comparatively recent accomplishment. Blood transfusions and "intravenous" injections are commonplace now, but in the early twentieth century, they were fraught with danger. A surgeon was obviously the right person to do it. So, as Fleming was a trained surgeon, he was the one to take it up. Fleming also had no private practice to lose or reputation to ruin if anything went wrong.

But the drug was successful in the treatment of syphilis and further developments in the same series were even more so. Immediately it was tried on all sorts of other illnesses, but of those occurring in our climate, none were cured by it.

Wright was not unduly worried by this success. Here was only a single exception to his rule about stimulating immunity being the only right way to cure or prevent disease. But for Fleming, it was something to think about. However his chief might explain it away, the Old Man had been shown to be wrong. A chemical could work effectively—and safely—inside the body.

TEXT-DEPENDENT QUESTIONS

1. What allergists worked with Almroth Wright?
2. Who was the first person to show that germs cause disease?
3. What is immunology?

RESEARCH PROJECT

Using your school library or the internet, find out more about one of the notable scientists mentioned in this chapter, including: Antonie van Leeuwenhoek, Agostino Bassi, Louis Pasteur, Casimir Joseph Davaine, Robert Koch, Elie Metchnikoff, or Paul Ehrlich. Write a two-page report about this scientist's life and accomplishments, and present your findings to the class.

View of the casino and beach at Boulogne, France, where a bacteriology laboratory was established for Fleming and the rest of Wright's research team during the First World War.

8081. P. Z - BOULOGNE - SUR - MER. LA PLAGE ET LE CASINO

 WORDS TO UNDERSTAND

antibiotic—a chemical produced by a living organism, such as penicillium mold, that destroys other bacteria.

asepsis—careful technique to avoid introducing infection.

bactericidal—a substance that kills bacteria; this can be an ordinary chemical or one made by the body.

enzyme—a chemical made in a living cell that acts on other substances to break them down by digesting them, or to build them up into new substances.

phagocytosis—the process of eating up bacteria.

tetanus—also called "lockjaw," a spasm of muscles due to the toxin of the tetanus bacterium, *Clostridium tetani*.

CHAPTER 3

War and Aftermath

War broke out in August 1914. By this time Wright's vaccines were being used against typhoid fever, which in the Boer War had been responsible for more casualties than all the bullets of the Boer farmers. Vaccines were also being used against a number of other diseases with great success. In fact, Wright's typhoid vaccine was so successful (in the First World War only 0.24 percent of British soldiers caught typhoid, compared to over 10 percent during the Boer War) that after the war, he was knighted for his efforts and persistence in pressing for its use.

In 1914, however, the War Office decided it did not need any bacteriologists—only ordinary doctors. Wright's team was disbanded and, as they were mostly former officers—or else, like Fleming and Freeman, territorials—they were sent into the army as battalion medical officers.

It soon became clear that the bacteria were working for the enemy, on both sides. Wounded soldiers were dying in hospitals of infection. Gangrene infections and **tetanus** were responsible for perhaps as much as 10 percent of all the deaths. The old team was recalled. Wright, given the rank of colonel, was sent out to Boulogne to set up a new unit for the study of war wounds. Captain Douglas and Fleming, now a lieutenant, went with him, and Leonard Colebrook followed later. John Freeman was sent first to Russia to prepare cholera vaccines, and afterward on to Boulogne. The research center was set up at the Casino and established as the 13th General Hospital. They had as their liaison officer a Frenchman, André Maurois, who described them in *The Silences of Colonel*

Bramble and a number of other books. Years later he became Fleming's official biographer.

Again, Wright's group worked as a team and their publications were joint ones. Their experiences must have been horrifying and had a profound effect. They were a fairly tough bunch, used to examining dead bodies in the postmortem room, but they would never talk about what they went through in Boulogne, nor did they ever use their experiences there to illustrate their teaching. Fleming and Colebrook never stopped working on infection, burns, and wounds for the rest of their lives.

An Important Discovery

It was at Boulogne that Fleming conducted a series of brilliant experiments that showed that antiseptic chemicals, when wrongly used, could be dangerous or were, at the very best, useless in fighting infection.

Surgeons since the time of Lister had been very enthusiastic about antiseptics, and their use spread from surgery to general hospital sterilization and even to the dressing of wounds. All this had become standard teaching, or conventional wisdom. "I remember," Fleming said, "that I used to be told to be most careful to use antiseptics in the dressing of wounds—carbolic acid, boric acid, peroxide of hydrogen. I could see for myself that these antiseptics did not kill all the microbes, but was told that they killed some, and that the results were better than if no antiseptics had been used at all. At that time I was in no position to argue."

What Fleming's experiments at the Casino showed, however, was that not only did some antiseptics that he used fail to attack infections like gangrene, they actually made things worse! If he put antiseptic chemicals into a wound, they would kill more of the defending white cells than the invading germs. He found

Opposite page: World War I medics give first aid on the battlefield in France. During the war (1914–18), Fleming served as a captain in the Royal Army Medical Corps, mostly at battlefield hospitals in France.

that there was only one chemical that did not do more harm than good. This was hypochlorite solution known as Eusol (Edinburgh University Solution), and sold today as household bleach. As far as Wright was concerned, all chemicals for killing bacteria were a failure inside the body. Their place was, precisely, in drains and sinks and Fleming's experiments confirmed this view.

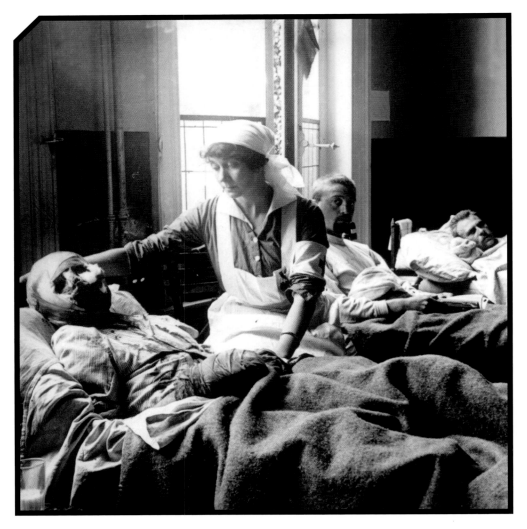

A nurse cares for an injured Allied soldier in a hospital in Antwerp, Belgium.

It had become—and still is—normal practice in surgery to use "no-touch" techniques, working carefully to avoid contamination, and to sterilize everything used during an operation if there is to be any hope of a clean, germ-free result. This is known as **asepsis**. But the very success in surgery and hospital medicine of both asepsis and antisepsis became a barrier to further progress, and herein lies a lesson. As soon as a scientific idea is accepted automatically and no longer thought about, it becomes as dangerous as a superstition.

After the War

Once the war was over, the group was brought back together again at St. Mary's Hospital, Paddington. Before the war they had been totally under Wright's control, working on the problems that interested him. Now they were more experienced scientists looking for a chance to follow up their own ideas. But Wright still wanted and needed them, so places had to be found for each of them at the hospital.

His old friend Captain Douglas presented no problems. He went as director to the Medical Research Council's laboratories. The rest of them had to set up their own lines of research. John Freeman went into practice as an allergist and

IN FLANDERS FIELDS MUSEUM
YPRES, BELGIUM

Scan here to learn more about battlefield medicine during the first World War.

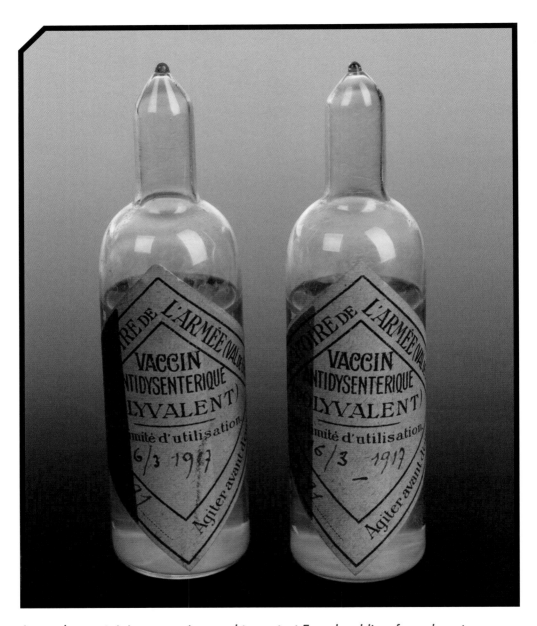

Ampoules containing a vaccine used to protect French soldiers from dysentery, produced in 1917. The disease affects the small intestine, causing diarrhea and vomiting, and is spread through contaminated food and water. It was important to immunize soldiers against dysentery in order to maintain a fit and healthy fighting force.

supported research into the subject largely out of his own pocket. He built up huge hay fever and asthma clinics at the hospital. He was from then on constantly played off against his colleague Fleming, with the promise that when Wright retired (a thing he never intended to do anyway), Freeman would be head of the new Institute that Wright had founded.

The income of the institute, like the Pasteur and Lister Institutes, depended on the sale of its vaccines, and this became Fleming's territory. An American firm, Parke Davis, was the only drug house that would market them. The money earned in this way not only had to support research but also to pay for the diagnostic work of the hospital, for the teaching of bacteriology, and for the rest of the hospital's work on disease.

Fleming was also involved on the teaching side and he had now been given the title of Professor. His new status did not, however, give him any greater control of the funds of the institute, nor did he find himself more able to influence its policy, but at least he now had a small room of his own (on the turret stairs under the library) and research students to work with him.

Leonard Colebrook worked closely with Wright for a time, but he left the department when the chance came to take up full time research as Director of the Bernard Baron Institute at Queen Charlotte's Maternity Hospital. Building up a brilliant research team mainly, though not entirely, drawn from the next generation of St. Mary's students, he set them to work on infections in mothers and babies and developed safer methods of childbirth. He was, later on, to play a very important part in the development of drugs against bacteria and remained throughout his career on friendly terms with the group at St. Mary's.

Nature's Antiseptic

Although Fleming's day was made up of routine work and teaching, his spare time was now his own and he used it to follow up his own ideas. Up to now he had been very influential in getting people to understand that, in general, chemicals could not be used safely inside the body. Now he was to make one of his great, and apparently casual, observations that was to overthrow this position and clear the way for the great advance of **antibiotics**.

Of all bacteriologists at that time, Fleming knew most about the action of antiseptics in the body. Without doubt, he believed they were harmful. One of them, however, had worked: 606 (salvarsan) and a better version, neosalvarsan.

In the story of the next observation, again something happens that was not planned. Indeed, it could not have been foreseen in any way.

One winter day, Fleming was examining some bacterial colonies growing on a culture plate. He had a runny nose, and some mucus accidentally dripped onto the culture plate. The bacterial colonies had not been planted there by Fleming but had come by accident from the air. They were contaminants. He noticed that the colonies that had been splashed by the mucus melted away, but the other colonies were not affected.

At once Fleming set out a beautiful series of experiments to show where the substance dissolving the bacteria was present in the human body, and also

SCIENTIFIC COLLECTOR

Fleming never threw anything away. One scientist who worked with him later said that in 1958, the medical staff was working to clean up supplies leftover from the Second World War, which had ended thirteen years earlier. Test tubes, their once white cotton wool plugs black with the dust of the blitz and the soot from Paddington station, were being cleared out of Fleming's cupboards. He rescued some from the wastepaper baskets saying, "Don't throw them away, they are my pike's eggs and kangaroo tendons." He kept them until there was an exhibition of work in the laboratory, and used them yet again to show that another spell in a test tube in a cupboard had not weakened the enzyme.

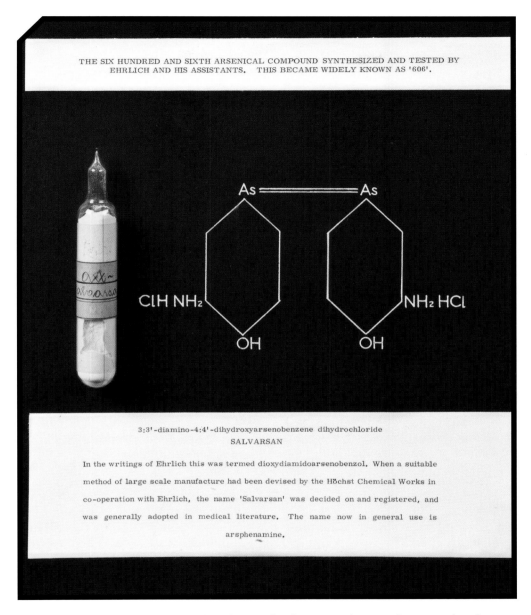

THE SIX HUNDRED AND SIXTH ARSENICAL COMPOUND SYNTHESIZED AND TESTED BY EHRLICH AND HIS ASSISTANTS. THIS BECAME WIDELY KNOWN AS '606'.

3:3'-diamino-4:4'-dihydroxyarsenobenzene dihydrochloride
SALVARSAN

In the writings of Ehrlich this was termed dioxydiamidoarsenobenzol. When a suitable method of large scale manufacture had been devised by the Höchst Chemical Works in co-operation with Ehrlich, the name 'Salvarsan' was decided on and registered, and was generally adopted in medical literature. The name now in general use is arsphenamine.

This display shows the chemical makeup of salvarsan, along with a sample of the drug, which appears like a yellow powder. The drug was also known as 606 because it was the six hundred and sixth compound tested in German scientist Paul Ehrlich's laboratory. First synthesized in 1907 and used to treat syphilis, the drug today is known as Arsphenamine.

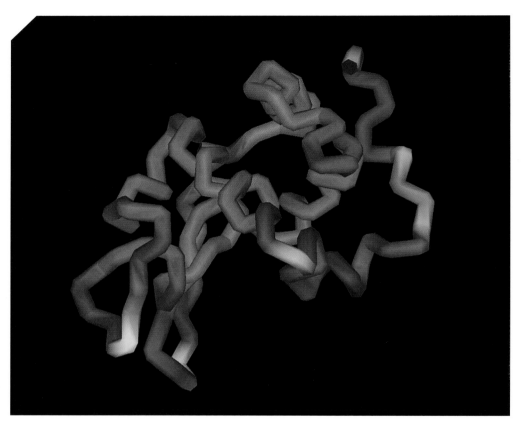

Molecular model of human lysozyme. This is an enzyme that is involved in the destruction of the sugar chains that make up some bacterial cell walls.

how widely it was to be found in nature. He found it in all the body fluids and in almost every body tissue. He also had the help of the zoo at Regent's Park. When one of their animals died and had a postmortem examination, various parts of its body were sent to him.

His final conclusion was that this substance, called "lysozyme" at Wright's suggestion, was an **enzyme**—a substance vital to certain bodily chemical changes, and an important part of the body's defenses against disease. It is also what keeps eggs free of germs. He published his first paper on lysozyme with a research student at St. Mary's, V. D. Allison, in 1922 and finally summarized the work in a presidential address to the pathology section of the Royal Society of Medicine ten years later. At this meeting he was able to show that the pike's eggs he had used ten years before to demonstrate the effects of lysozyme for his earlier paper were still as active and effective as ever.

The source of lysozyme for Fleming's early experiments was human tears. They were clean and easily collected by seizing a passing student or laboratory boy and dropping lemon juice in his eye. Scientists eventually turned to collecting the substance from egg whites, because they have a stronger concentration of lysozyme than tears.

The discovery of lysozyme did not help directly in the treatment of disease. Everyone has enough lysozyme in his body to kill any germ that is affected by it. It has been, however, of great value in dissolving germs so that they can be studied chemically, and it is now a standard research tool. The papers Fleming wrote were important in other ways.

For him, and us, the value of this work was twofold—first in method and second in thought. He needed methods that would measure differences in sensitivity to lysozyme of various microbes using only a very small amount of lysozyme. He used a method of diffusion. He made holes, or wells, with a cork borer in the jelly in his culture plates, and filled them with a solution of lysozyme. The various germs to be tested would be spread around the holes. Their sensitivity to lysozyme would be measured by how far away from the hole they were killed. Indeed, almost all the methods we now use in testing antibiotics were developed from Fleming's tests on lysozyme.

Perhaps more important was the change in Fleming's thinking about chemicals in the body. He stated the case himself in his 1932 presidential address, "I think I am correct in saying that in 1921 most bacteriologists agreed with the quotation from Metchnikoff:

"Nature, to protect the skin and mucous membranes, does not use antiseptics. The fluids which bathe the surface of the mouth and other mucous membranes are not bactericidal, or only very imperfectly so. Nature removes from the mucous membranes and the skin quantities of microbes, eliminating them by epithelial desquamation and expelling them with the secretions and liquid excretions.

Nature has chosen this mechanical procedure. . . .' " (Epithelial desquamation means "the flaking-off of skin.")

Fleming then continued with his own comment: "The work which has been done in connection with lysozyme has certainly caused us to modify our views in this respect and has shown that quite apart from **phagocytosis** and the **bactericidal** power of the blood fluids, the tissues and secretions have also some primary antiseptic properties."

The term "phagocytosis" that he uses here means the "eating up" of germs by the white cells of the blood. The bactericidal power of the fluids is the killing of germs by blood without any white cells taking part. It is clear that Fleming had now arrived at the idea that there might well be chemical substances that would kill bacteria without harming the body's own cells. The idea was not really new, as two special examples were already known. Quinine was used against malaria, and salvarsan, as Fleming's own experience had shown, worked well in curing syphilis. Neither of these showed any very bad effects on the patient, though they were by no means perfect. But Fleming, like the other people of his time, had thought of these as odd exceptions.

Fleming now began to accept the general idea of safe chemicals killing germs in the body. This, together with the new techniques he had worked out for testing lysozyme, put him in an ideal position to take advantage of his next observation. Chance was ready to play its trump card.

TEXT-DEPENDENT QUESTIONS

1. In what year did the First World War begin?
2. What is asepsis?
3. Where did Leonard Colebrook go when he left St. Mary's?

RESEARCH PROJECT

The horrors spawned by World War I weren't confined to the battlefield. Civilians, too, suffered enormously. Sometimes the harm they endured was unintended, but sometimes they were deliberately targeted. Perhaps no episode was more notorious (or remains more controversial today) than the Ottoman Empire's treatment of its Armenian minority. Use the internet to find out what happened to the Armenians of Turkey beginning in April 1915. Write a one-page report.

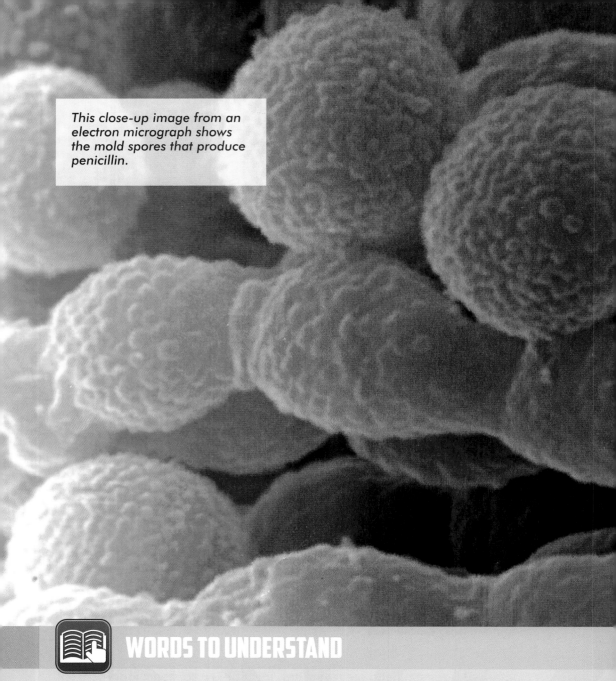

This close-up image from an electron micrograph shows the mold spores that produce penicillin.

WORDS TO UNDERSTAND

colony—a group of bacterial cells growing together, usually all coming from the same parent cell.

mycologist—someone who studies molds and fungi.

staphylococcus—a spherical bacterium that forms grape-like clusters.

CHAPTER 4

The Discovery of Penicillin

With the identification of lysozome, Fleming was convinced that he had made a discovery of immense importance. However, his series of superb studies on the matter had raised little excitement in the medical world. Fleming soon busied himself with fresh experiments to explore new ideas.

By September 1928, he was investigating the range of variation in a certain type of bacterium called **staphylococcus**—trying to find out in what ways individual bacterium of the same type were different from each other. For example, at that time nothing was known about how bacteria reproduced, and nothing was known about their patterns of heredity. Yet it was clear from slight alterations in color or shape between different **colonies** of the same type that not all individuals were alike.

These differences seemed important to Fleming. He had managed in earlier experiments to change certain staphylococci in such a way that lysozyme could no longer kill them. How did this happen? Could every single bacterium of this type learn to resist lysozyme, or just a few special bacteria that would then pass on their ability by breeding a new population? This was the sort of question Fleming was asking. He hoped that his new series of experiments might give him some answers.

For this purpose, he was breeding several different strains of staphylococci. He would lift the lids of his culture plates from time to time, to check on how they were developing. While doing this one day, he noticed that one of the culture plates had developed a green mold. How annoying! It was now useless. He would have to throw it away. For the moment, however, he just put it to one side with some other dishes that had also been contaminated with various molds.

Tidiness was not one of Fleming's strong points. In those days, when a researcher finished using a culture plate, it was dropped into a dish full of antiseptic solution. This would kill any bacteria on them, and make them safe to handle by the technician who washed the dishes. By the time Fleming got around to returning his used dishes, however, the pile was so high that those on top were well clear of the antiseptic.

On that day, however, Merlin Pryce, who had been helping Fleming with his earlier experiments on variation in bacteria, dropped by to see how things were

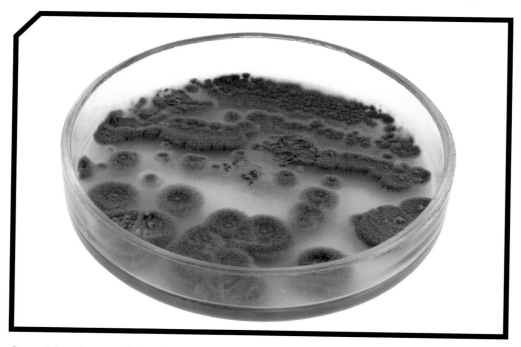

Greenish colonies of the fungus Penicillium *occurred from contamination by mold spores on a Petri dish, or culture plate. Fleming was a brilliant researcher, but a sloppy and chaotic lab technician. His carelessness leaving some cultures unattended led to the discovery of penicillin.*

A plaque outside St. Mary's Hospital in London marks the tower where Fleming's office was located, and where he made his famous discovery.

going. Fleming pointed to some of the plates he had thrown away. "As soon as you uncover a culture dish something tiresome is sure to happen," he said. "Things fall out of the air." Then something caught his eye in the plate with the green mold. All around the mold, the staphylococci colonies had disappeared. Everywhere else in the dish, they were flourishing. It appeared that the mold was producing something that was killing the staphylococci.

We now call that something "penicillin"—a drug that would revolutionize medicine. But Fleming did not know that at the time. Though he was excited by his find, his experience with antiseptics had made him unusually cautious. He jumped to no hasty conclusions, but went back to work.

The arrival of the mold in the Petri dish may have been most fortunate of accidents—but the next phase of the research required hard, careful work.

A HARD MAN TO KNOW

"Alexander Fleming was a man who did not wish to be known, who hid his views on everything except his work from all who came into contact with him," wrote his former St. Mary's colleague W. Howard Hughes. "He had little use for conversation and expressed himself only through the work of his hands and his experiments. His shyness was such that throughout his career he kept a barrier around himself that was rarely crossed, and only then by his more intimate friends."

To his colleagues at work, Hughes recalled, Fleming would make only the most fleeting reference to his home and family life, or to his hobbies. He was equally silent at the Savage Club, a gentlemen's club in London where he was a longtime member. Anyone who questioned him at the club about his work could expect only the shortest of answers. At home in Chelsea—when he was at home, for he spent most of his evenings in the laboratory—he would entertain his friends from the Chelsea Art Club, and at his house in the Suffolk countryside, where he spent his weekends and holidays, he would involve himself with his family, his gardening, games, and sports.

So completely did Fleming separate these sides to his life that he had three nicknames, one for each situation, and very few people knew more than one. At work, he was known as "Flem" or, occasionally by students and younger colleagues, "the Prof"; at home, he was called "Alec"; and at the club, he was known as "Sandy."

Fleming was ideally suited to the job. He was interested in natural antiseptics, and had unique experiences from his experiments with lysozyme. He tried all his lysozyme tricks, using the mold juice, and they worked perfectly. He tested its effect on a wide range of disease germs, leaving out only two major ones—tetanus and gangrene.

A Fortunate Accident

Fleming's own description of the discovery of penicillin is short. "While working with staphylococcal variants a number of culture-plates were set aside on the laboratory bench and examined from time to time," he later wrote. "In the examination these plates were necessarily exposed to the air and they became contaminated with various microorganisms. It was noticed that around a large **colony** of contaminating mold the staphylococcus colonies became transparent and were obviously undergoing lysis (cell destruction)."

How did the mold arrive on the culture plate? No one is certain. A popular explanation of the 1940s was that the mold had been blown into Fleming's lab through the open windows. This explanation is highly unlikely, however. Bacteriologists do not usually work with open windows, and, according to his St.

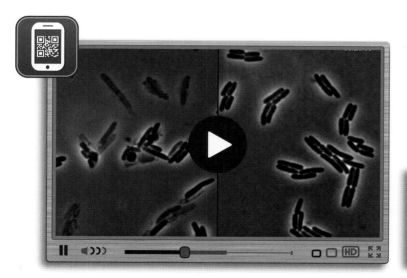

Scan here to see bacteria being killed by penicillin:

Mary's colleagues, Fleming never did. In any case, the window in his laboratory was difficult to open, and could only be reached by leaning over the lab table, where there was a Bunsen burner and several hot water baths.

A more likely explanation is related to other researchers who worked in the turret at St. Mary's where Fleming had his laboratory. The room immediately underneath Fleming's was occupied by a **mycologist** named Charles J. La Touche. A mycologist is a specialist in molds and fungi of all sorts, from toadstools right down to cells not much larger than bacteria.

La Touche had been brought into the department by John Freeman. Freeman had originally been interested in studying hay fever and asthma due to grass pollen. His attention had now turned to "dust asthma," which he thought might be due to mold spores in damp houses. For his research, he wanted a large bulk of mold spores from his patients' own homes. With these, Freeman made extracts to test on their skin.

Mycologists at that time were not used to handling organisms that were known to cause disease in man. They were less careful in their methods and did not feel worried if some of the spore cultures were spilled or shaken into the air. There were probably more mold spores in the air of St. Mary's laboratories at that time than ever before or since. It is very likely that the famous mold arrived on Fleming's culture plate that way.

Fleming believed that the mold got onto his plate when he lifted its lid to look at it. However, this is probably not true for a number of reasons. Most important is that the mold does not immediately start to produce penicillin. Only when it has developed into a fairly large colony do the drops of yellow fluid begin to appear on the surface and spread over the culture plate or into the flask of broth, and this takes about five days. Also, penicillin acts on bacterial cell walls in such a way that it only works while the bacteria (staphylococci, in this case) are still growing. After growth has stopped, the bacteria cannot be killed.

The staphylococci that Fleming was growing on the culture plate would normally stop dividing in about eighteen hours when kept at the normal temperature of the human body, 98.6°F (37°C). If Fleming had not taken the moldy plate out of the incubator, the mold juice would not have killed the bacteria. An incubator can be

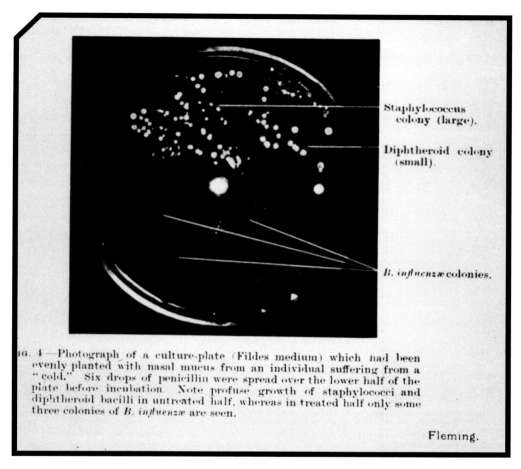

Staphylococcus colony (large).

Diphtheroid colony (small).

B. influenzæ colonies.

ᵢ₆. 4—Photograph of a culture-plate (Fildes medium) which had been evenly planted with nasal mucus from an individual suffering from a "cold." Six drops of penicillin were spread over the lower half of the plate before incubation. Note profuse growth of staphylococci and diphtheroid bacilli in untreated half, whereas in treated half only some three colonies of B. influenzæ are seen.

Fleming.

A photo reproduced in Fleming's original paper about penicillin shows how the mold inhibited the growth of influenza. The bottom half of the dish was pre-treated with penicillin, while the top was left untreated before the influenza germs were added. After an incubation period, the germs are flourishing at the top, but nearly nonexistent on the bottom half of the dish.

controlled, but bacterial growth at room temperature depends on the weather. The mold and the organism each had to grow at just the right rate, which in this case happened to be about 60°F (18°C). It was vital that the temperature did not rise above this level for nearly a week. Although the plate disposal occurred during the first week in August, it was unusually chilly for that

Reprinted from
The British Journal of Experimental Pathology,
1929, Vol. X, p. 226.

ON THE ANTIBACTERIAL ACTION OF CULTURES OF A PENICILLIUM, WITH SPECIAL REFERENCE TO THEIR USE IN THE ISOLATION OF *B. INFLUENZAE.*

ALEXANDER FLEMING, F.R.C.S.

From the Laboratories of the Inoculation Department, St. Mary's Hospital, London.

Received for publication May 10, 1929.

WHILE working with staphylococcus variants a number of culture-plates were set aside on the laboratory bench and examined from time to time. In the examinations these plates were necessarily exposed to the air and they became contaminated with various micro-organisms. It was noticed that around a large colony of a contaminating mould the staphylococcus colonies became transparent and were obviously undergoing lysis (see Fig. 1).

Subcultures of this mould were made and experiments conducted with a view to ascertaining something of the properties of the bacteriolytic substance which had evidently been formed in the mould culture and which had diffused into the surrounding medium. It was found that broth in which the mould had been grown at room temperature for one or two weeks had acquired marked inhibitory, bactericidal and bacteriolytic properties to many of the more common pathogenic bacteria.

CHARACTERS OF THE MOULD.

The colony appears as a white fluffy mass which rapidly increases in size and after a few days sporulates, the centre becoming dark green and later in old cultures darkens to almost black. In four or five days a bright yellow colour is produced which diffuses into the medium. In certain conditions a reddish colour can be observed in the growth.

In broth the mould grows on the surface as a white fluffy growth, changing in a few days to a dark green felted mass. The broth becomes bright yellow and this yellow pigment is not extracted by $CHCl_3$. The reaction of the broth becomes markedly alkaline. the pH varying from 8·5 to 9. Acid is produced in three or four days in glucose and saccharose broth. There is no acid production in 7 days in lactose, mannite or dulcite broth.

Growth is slow at 37°C. and is most rapid about 20°C. No growth is observed under anaerobic conditions.

In its morphology this organism is a penicillium and in all its characters it most closely resembles *P. rubrum.* Biourge (1923) states that he has never found *P. rubrum* in nature and that it is an " animal de laboratoire." This penicillium is not uncommon in the air of the laboratory.

IS THE ANTIBACTERIAL BODY ELABORATED IN CULTURE BY ALL MOULDS ?

A number of other moulds were grown in broth at room temperature and the culture fluids were tested for antibacterial substances at various intervals up to one month. The species examined were : *Eidamia viridiscens, Botrytis cineria, Aspergillus fumigatus, Sporotrichum, Cladosporium, Penicillium,* 8 strains. Of these it was found

1

Fleming's original paper on penicillin, published in the British Journal of Experimental Pathology *in 1929.*

time of year, and the temperature in Fleming's lab, incredibly, did not rise above that critical level.

Thus a series of accidents had to happen to make the discovery of penicillin possible. Out of all the molds that occur in nature, how many of them would have produced the effect he saw? Years later, after the Second World War, drug houses in many countries started a search for molds in all sorts of places: the fruit markets of the southern states of the United States, the forest floor in Central America, the sewage outflow of Mediterranean islands. It is guessed that at least a million had to be examined before a new and useful one was found. This would confirm the theory that the mold came from La Touche's downstairs laboratory. Fleming wrote that La Touche found him four more strains of penicillium that did the same thing. This must mean that he had plenty of material there. The strains could even have all come from the same house.

Initial Response to the Discovery

At first, Fleming's colleagues and other bacteriologists were not enthusiastic about his discovery. Fleming's first report was given to the Medical Research Club. This was a private group that held informal after-dinner meetings. For Fleming, this must have been a nightmarish occasion. The audience was filled with accomplished scientists and doctors. Fleming was shy and not a good public speaker, so it is easy to understand why they were not impressed. The members showed little interest, and did not discuss his findings at any length.

His great paper was published in a research journal, *The British Journal of Experimental Pathology*. This journal publishes quickly and accepts unusual papers. It has the drawback that its readership consists of other research workers, rather than doctors who work directly with patients. Nowadays such a paper would also be reported in a short form, an abstract, in journals that specialize in this; in those days, however, none existed.

His title was enough to put off any casual reader. It was "On the Antibacterial Action of Cultures of a Penicillium, with special reference to their use in the isolation of *B. influenzae*." Fleming reported only facts that he could show had an immediate, practical laboratory use. He was not prepared to speculate, or claim any benefits that he could not fully prove. But he certainly saw the possibilities of the mold juice. Following are the points Fleming made in his paper:

1. A certain type of penicillium mold produces, when cultured, a powerful substance that kills bacteria. This antibacterial power reaches its maximum strength in about seven days when grown at 20°C [68°F], and after ten days starts to get less and less until it has almost disappeared after four weeks.

2. The growth medium that has best produced the antibacterial substance is ordinary nutrient broth.

3. The active ingredient can be filtered off easily, and the name "penicillin" has been given to it.

4. The action is very marked against the pus-forming bacteria and the diphtheria group of bacilli. Many bacteria, however, are quite insensitive to it.

5. Penicillin is not poisonous to animals, even in enormous doses, nor is it an irritant. It does not interfere with the action of the white cells in the blood.

6. It is suggested that it may be a good antiseptic to use against penicillin-sensitive microbes in the body.

7. The use of penicillin on culture plates brings to light the way in which bacteria may interfere with others. This is not very evident in ordinary cultures.

8. The value of penicillin isolating *B. influenzae* [a type of flu germ] has been demonstrated.

Fleming examines cultures in a Petri dish.

TEXT-DEPENDENT QUESTIONS

1. What type of bacterium was Fleming studying when he discovered penicillin?
2. Who was Charles J. La Touche?
3. Where was Fleming's major paper on penicillin published?

RESEARCH PROJECT

Try this simple method to produce penicillium mold. Take a medium-sized orange, and poke it with a fork a few times so that juice runs out. Put it in a shallow dish, and leave it in a cool, dark place for seven to ten days. At the end of this period, the orange will be covered with a greenish mold. This mold is penicillium, and can be processed into penicillin.

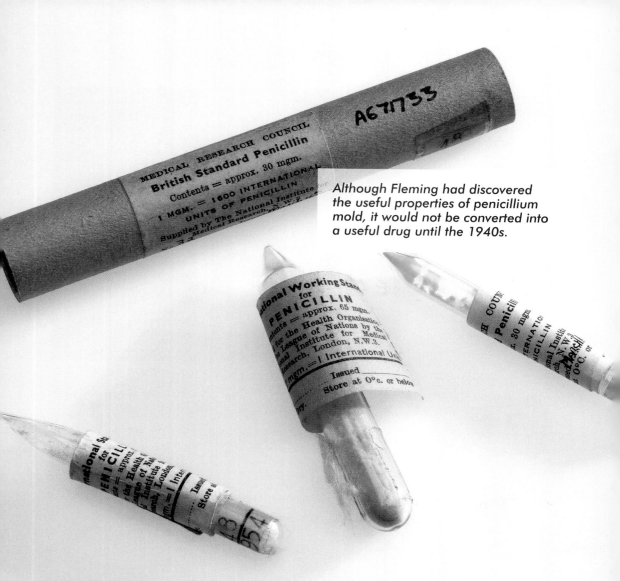

Although Fleming had discovered the useful properties of penicillium mold, it would not be converted into a useful drug until the 1940s.

 WORDS TO UNDERSTAND

chemotherapy—treatment by drugs or other chemicals.

globulin—part of the blood fluids responsible for the body's defenses.

potency—the strength of a drug or chemical.

streptococcus—a spherical bacterium that forms chains.

CHAPTER 5

The Period of Failure and Neglect

Fleming had made an important observation and worked out methods for culturing the penicillium mold. Obviously, his next step should have been to get hold of large amounts to continue experiments with laboratory animals and then with human patients. Why did he not do this? The answer is that penicillin is an unstable substance. It very quickly loses its **potency**. In the late 1920s, chemical methods that could stabilize such substances had not yet been developed. It was not because Fleming and his assistants did not want to isolate the drug, but that chemistry techniques had not progressed enough to make this possible.

A number of things had to happen before penicillin could be produced in useful amounts. The first was that the medical profession as a whole had to be persuaded to change its mind about the use of drugs to treat infection. The second was that new techniques in biochemistry had to be introduced. What finally did the trick was that a situation arose that made the government need a substance like penicillin so badly that it was prepared to spend a lot of money to get it.

Fleming initially tried to get Wright to put up the money for the chemical research that would be needed to develop penicillin. But Wright was rather biased against chemists. He disliked the idea that, one day, the active ingredients of blood that were responsible for immunity might be seen to be chemical substances. He insisted on thinking of them as "functions" of the blood. Nowadays proteins in the blood that help the human immune system are well known. Most of them are what are called **globulins**.

There were no proper chemists in the bacteriology department at St. Mary's, and none—even among the medical school's chemistry teachers—who could, or would, attempt to prepare pure penicillin. The only help that could be found was given by two young men, Frederick Ridley and Stuart Craddock, who had some chemical knowledge. They were given a sink and draining board in a corridor just outside the laboratory. Their studies almost led to a stable preparation, but the final step was beyond them.

When they had done their best and failed, Fleming tried to get help from other laboratories in the University of London system. These efforts also failed, either because the chemists got no help from their own bacteriologists, or because there was no real enthusiasm for the work.

So at this stage Fleming was left with another substance that, like lysozyme, had no clinical uses. Many years later, Fleming said, "I had failed for want of adequate chemical help. Raistrick and his associates had lacked bacteriological cooperation." He was referring to Doctor Harold Raistrick, a professor of biochemistry who worked at the London School of Tropical Medicine and Hygiene. At Fleming's urging, Raistrick had tried to produce a pure form of penicillin, but had only limited success.

Teaching and Studying

For the next six years, Fleming and his mold were forgotten. He wrote a few articles for textbooks, but published little that was new. He shelved his work on penicillin and took up other duties. The drug would have to wait for other men to make it famous.

Fleming's spent his time on the usual duties of a university professor. He did some organizing, some teaching, and some diagnostic work for hospital patients as well as his own patients. Apart from these routine duties, he spent a lot of his time testing and improving the department's vaccines. This was a special interest of his, for the entire research program of the institute depended on the sale of these vaccines.

Another of Fleming's interests during this period was in the way one type of living microbe interferes with others. He did a great deal of work to find out how one particular germ could be selected for study by suppressing others that were in its company. For this he took advantage of his knowledge of resistance and sensitivity to penicillin and crude chemicals such as the dyes. He was not alone in this. The modern methods of selection on which so much present-day diagnosis depends were the result of a broad advance by his colleagues all over the world.

Fleming examines a bacteria culture in a Petri dish. He was forty-eight years old when he published his paper on penicillin.

The sort of problem that interference between microbes caused can be illustrated by an outbreak of diphtheria in a certain boys' school. At the same time as the diphtheria bacillus was going around, the school there was also an outbreak of infection with staphylococcus. In those boys with diphtheria alone, the diagnosis was made immediately, but in those who were infected with both germs, it was missed. Why? The reason is that when the two germs were put together on a culture plate, the staphylococcus stopped the diphtheria bacillus from growing. A missed diagnosis like this would not happen today. All laboratories now use the selective plates developed by bacteriologists in the 1930s.

The scale of the work had, by now, grown enormously. The institute moved out of the used hospital wards into a specially built suite of laboratories next to the new medical school. Here Fleming had a number of assistants who were loyal to him, rather than to the older generation represented by Wright. Much of the stimulus and many of the ideas for their work came from Fleming, but, unlike a traditional professor, he did not ask for his name to appear on the papers they wrote. He did not then, or at any time, search for fame or publicity. Before he would let anything be published, it had to be up to the standard he required. But if their research met his standard, as long as it was known to come from his department, Fleming did not look for any credit for himself. Years later, after he became director of the institute, he explained that this was a reaction to Wright, who believed the head of a department should be mentioned in everything that his department published.

Fleming pointed out that the department's "tea parties" were for the exchange

BACTERIA "GAMES"

Alexander Fleming did not always help his reputation with the ways that he presented his discoveries, according to his St. Mary's colleague and biographer W. Howard Hughes. "He never liked to blow up an observation or experiment into a published paper," wrote Hughes. "He far preferred to make his points by pretty little demonstrations at laboratory meetings. He presented the results of his work on microbe selection by making drawings on filter paper with a mixture of differently colored bacteria. If the filter paper turned out to be yellow, this meant that the yellow bacteria were stopping the others growing. When he dripped onto the filter paper a chemical that killed only the yellow bacteria red or purple ones would grow in their place. This was meant to put an important point simply and visually. Instead, his critics saw it only as a game with bacteria and nothing else."

of ideas. These could be thrown into the conversation by anyone. They were improved and altered through discussion, until they finally appeared in a form that suggested an experiment. Fleming insisted that the credit should not go to the person who had the first idea, or started the conversation, but to the person who did the hard work in the laboratory to prove or disprove it.

Changing Attitudes

Over this period the whole attitude to **chemotherapy** was coming around to Fleming's viewpoint. This change was brought about not by him, but by his old friend Leonard Colebrook at Queen Charlotte's Maternity Hospital. Colebrook had been working with a small but brilliant team on infection in women who had babies. This disease, puerperal fever, is a form of blood poisoning by bacteria. Up to one in ten mothers who came into the hospital to have their babies caught it, and many died every year.

The bacteria that cause this disease are **streptococci**, round or oval germs arranged like beads on a thread. Colebrook's attention was drawn to a German paper that suggested that a red dye, prontosil, could cure mice of streptococcal infections. Might this work on the sick mothers? First he showed

Leonard Colebrook (1883–1967), a member of Wright's team before and during the First World War, moved after the war to Queen Charlotte's Maternity Hospital where he made great advances in the treatment of puerperal fever.

Howard Walter Florey (1898–1968), the Australian-born pathologist, was professor of pathology at Oxford from 1935 to 1962.

that it was successful in killing the streptococci causing the disease. It was then found out that the dye itself was not needed, only a certain colorless ingredient. This was just as well. It stopped everything about the patient being stained bright red! This ingredient, suphanilamide, turned out to be the first good drug that could be used in medicine since salvarsan, twenty-five years before.

Colebrook called on Fleming, who knew all the techniques, and asked him to find out how sulfanilamide worked. Fleming discovered that it did no harm to blood cells, and found a most interesting fact: it could not kill germs without them. It stopped the germs from multiplying, but the white cells of the blood had to do the killing.

This new chemical, and others that were soon made from it, changed the thinking of doctors. At last they were ready to consider other possible killers of bacteria. The stage was now set for the second entrance of penicillin. A key figure in penicillin's reemergence was a refugee from Hitler's Germany, a young chemist named Ernst Chain.

Oxford University had in 1935 appointed a smart young Australian as Professor of Pathology. His name was Howard Florey. He believed that bacteriology needed chemists to complete the work started by the bacteriologists, so he was soon on the lookout for a biochemist. He went for help and advice to Professor Gowland Hopkins at Cambridge, whose department was housing some refugees from Germany. Chain was introduced to Florey and joined his team.

Florey quickly followed up his idea of the need for chemical skill in bacteriology. He sent out everyone he could find, including the medical students, to hunt through library books to find any incomplete work that was worth pushing further. Chain started work with a young bacteriologist called Duthie. He worked first on chemicals produced by the body during inflammation. After that, he investigated lysozyme and showed that it was in fact an enzyme. His third substance was penicillin.

Chain used the results that had been published by Fleming and his team, and added his own chemical knowledge. He had no difficulty in producing a dry brown powder that did not lose its potency after a few days.

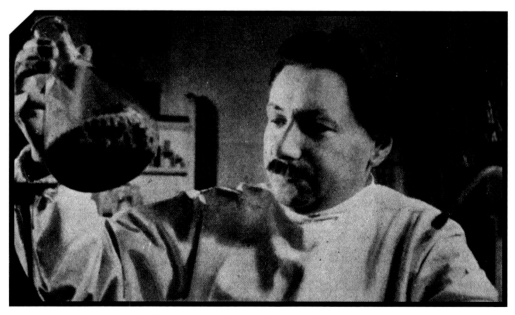

Ernst Chain (1906–79), the German-born chemist who fled to Britain from Nazi Germany in 1933. For his role in successfully preparing penicillin in a stable form, Chain shared the Nobel Prize for Medicine in 1945 with Fleming and Florey.

Photo of the Oxford team that worked to develop antibiotics, including (front, left to right) P. Fredericq and Maurice Welsch, (back) Selman Waksman, Howard Florey, Jacques Trefouel, Ernst Chain, and André Gratia.

On the morning of May 25, 1940, Florey tested the powder on four white Swiss mice that he had infected with streptococci. He infected four more mice in the same way, but these he did not treat with the penicillin that Chain had so carefully prepared. By three o'clock the next morning, all four of the second batch of mice were dead. All four that had been given penicillin, however, were still alive. Florey and Chain were thrilled. They immediately made plans for more experiments, and for increasing the production of penicillin by all possible means.

The results of Florey and Chain's experiments were published in August 1940, in *The Lancet*, a respected British medical journal. The paper was entitled "Penicillin as a Chemotherapeutic Agent." At the time, Chain did not know that Fleming was still alive. But he was.

Fleming was delighted at this new interest in his discovery, even when all the public credit was originally given to the Oxford team with no mention of Fleming. Wright, however, would not stand for one of his own people being overlooked in this way, even though he did not like the chemical approach. He wrote a letter to *The Times*, and made it quite clear where the original work had been done.

It is worth thinking about and comparing Fleming's and the Oxford team's contribution toward giving the world penicillin. It tells us something about the way

Scan here to learn how antibiotics work:

Glass fermentation vessels like this one were used in laboratories to produce penicillin in the early 1940s. The penicillium mold was grown on the surface of a liquid, filled with all the nutrients it needed. This approach was later replaced by the method of growing the mold within large industrial fermenters, allowing it to be mass produced.

that scientific knowledge increases today. With men like Louis Pasteur, Edward Jenner, and Joseph Lister, the great discoveries were the result of one man's efforts in following up what was often chance observation. Since then, the trend has been toward groups of research workers, no one of whom could claim all the credit for a discovery or its development. Their research is often a planned investigation of a chosen field.

Fleming's own description of himself as a Victorian naturalist with a modern microscope of course ignores his skill at investigating and exploring the things he ran across. Chain, on this occasion, was acting as a skilled chemist using his special knowledge on an existing problem—how to make a penicillin extract that could be kept active for some time. But lucky observations were not now a thing of the past. Chain himself was able to make one. He showed this when he was trying to grow a disease of rye, the fungus ergot, which is also a source of important drugs. However hard he tried, he just could not find a strain that would grow in deep broth cultures. One Sunday afternoon he recognized the symptoms of the disease in some rye grass growing by the side of a picnic spot where he was with his family. This gave him the culture he needed.

 ## TEXT-DEPENDENT QUESTIONS

1. What are globulins?
2. Why was the diphtheria bacillus not found in boys who also had been exposed to staphylococcus?
3. What useful drug did Leonard Colebrook discover?
4. Where were the results of Florey's and Chain's experiments with penicillin published?

 ## RESEARCH PROJECT

Using the internet or your school library, find out more about Howard Florey. Write a two-page paper on his life and accomplishments, and present it to your class.

Penicillin was a life-saving drug for Allied wounded during the Second World War. This photo shows the culture bottles in which penicillin was mass-produced, and small ampoules of the drug used by doctors and battlefield medics.

![WORDS TO UNDERSTAND]

WORDS TO UNDERSTAND

patent—an government license that allows a person who has made a scientific or industrial discovery to benefit from that discovery, by preventing others from using it without permission and/or payment.

toxin—a poisonous substance made by microbes.

toxoid—a modified toxin that can be used to prevent disease.

CHAPTER 6

Penicillin and the Second World War

Fleming's reaction to the new situation was at once to place the resources of St. Mary's Hospital at the disposal of the Oxford team. St. Mary's had a factory on the third floor of the building, and another in the basement, where vaccines were being produced for British military. By that time Great Britain was heavily engaged in the Second World War, which had begun when the armies of Nazi Germany invaded Poland in September 1939. St. Mary's had the capability to grow larger amounts of the helpful mold than Oxford could. Penicillin in its crude form in broth was poured off into large barrels, and put onto the passenger trains at Paddington to be collected at Oxford only about an hour later by their technicians.

This help was fully repaid when penicillin began being produced for clinical use. The first civilian patient whose life was saved by penicillin treatment given by Fleming was a police sergeant injured in the Blitz. Florey later let Fleming have the entire stock to treat a friend of his with a brain infection. This was the first time penicillin was injected into the spine.

Fleming was able to draw government attention to penicillin here, as on the committee of the institute were the Minister of Supply and an important industrialist. He was the wrong sort of person to influence government departments directly, however. Florey, on the other hand, had the right approach and succeeded in obtaining official American support. It was decided that production should be out of reach of the bombs that were then falling on British industrial towns, so the bulk of penicillin production would be carried out in the United States.

The war naturally took up the scientific resources at St. Mary's and all the university departments. Fleming was responsible, as Deputy Director, for the supervision of vaccine production. The small "factory" at St. Mary's had produced enough tetanus **toxoid** to immunize, through the Red Cross organization, both sides in the Spanish Civil War. Tetanus **toxin** is the poison made by the bacteria that cause tetanus. It is altered to a harmless form called a "toxoid," for immunization. This showed that particular tragedy of the First World War could be avoided. The factory was now expanded to produce, in addition to tetanus toxoid, injections against typhoid and cholera, diphtheria, whooping cough, and influenza, in case of another global pandemic like the one that followed the First World War.

War Work

Fleming's next responsibility was as sector pathologist. Southern England was divided into ten areas, like slices of a cake, the sharp point of each slice being at a London teaching hospital. Fleming's sector stretched from Paddington along the roads and railways running westward to Basingstoke, Winchester, and Southampton.

Pathologists were sent to set up laboratories to serve these areas and to look after the air raid casualties as they occurred, and later, to accept casualties straight from the invasion beaches of Europe on and after D-Day.

The war did not go at all as expected and the population of London stayed put. This meant that the central London hospitals had to be reopened, not just as casualty clearing stations as had been planned, but with proper outpatient

Opposite page: This World War II-era advertisement, which originally appeared in Life *magazine, calls penicillin "the greatest healing agent of this war."*

Thanks to PENICILLIN
...He Will Come Home!

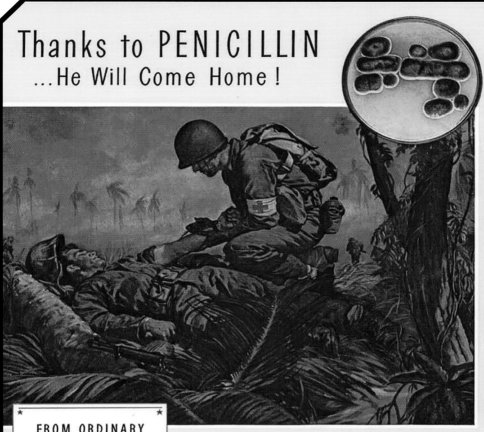

departments and wards to deal with ordinary illness and injury. Half the students were brought back to the hospitals to help with the work there, acting not only as dressers as they normally did, but also as stretcher bearers, fire watchers and unqualified house officers. They still needed teaching and courses were run at the

MEDICAL PATENTS

Before the Second World War, one of the foundational beliefs of British medical ethics was that there should be no secret remedies. Medical researchers generally did not seek to **patent** their ideas— to secure government protection that would prevent others from using them so that they could profit from them. The term "patent medicine" was almost a term of abuse and was usually taken to mean something dishonest or useless. When Colebrook and his team isolated sulfanilamide, they could have obtained a patent for their research institution, but Colebrook and his colleagues considered that unethical. In the same way, anyone could copy and sell the vaccines produced by St. Mary's; only the brand names were protected.

Fleming could have become extremely wealthy if he had decided to control and license penicillin. However, he believed that the world should benefit from its potential to cure diseases. He turned over the right to produce penicillin to the U.S. and British governments, so they could use it to treat people wounded in the Second World War. Neither Oxford nor St. Mary's gained any financial advantage from their discoveries related to penicillin.

After the war ended, the British Government arranged to hold patents on any discoveries made in universities and similar places. Today, university research laboratories receive patent payments when others utilize their discoveries.

Scan here to show how penicillin was mass-produced during the war:

safe provincial hospitals as well as the far-from-safe London ones by staffs that were already working flat out on emergency services.

There was a committee of sector pathologists, whose job was not only to run the service but also to provide up-to-date advice on all aspects of laboratory work for pathologists in the armed services, the Emergency Medical Service and the Public Health Laboratory Service. Here Fleming's skill in the laboratory and his Scottish thriftiness fit in with the needs of the time. Methods and results that in peacetime would have been given full-scale publication were just thrown out in news sheets and became known everywhere long before they were properly published. It was under these sorts of condition that the standard antibiotic disc, for showing whether a germ is sensitive before the patient is given any drugs, was invented. It soon became the standard method used all over the world to give a quick guide to treatment.

Recognition at Last

Fleming and Florey were both knighted in June 1944. The next year, Fleming, Florey, and Chain shared the Nobel Prize for Medicine. In the Nobel lecture

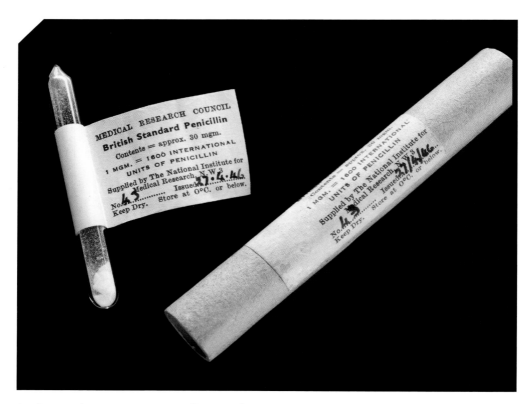

A glass vial containing penicillin, produced in the mid-1940s

that Fleming gave, he said, referring to the large scale production of penicillin that he had seen in America, "to me it was of especial interest to see how a simple observation made in a hospital bacteriological laboratory in London had eventually developed into a large industry, and how what everyone thought was merely one of my toys had, by purification, become the nearest approach to the ideal substance for curing many of our common infections."

Fleming himself expected that many more antibiotics would be found and that some of them would turn out to be better than his own.

The situation at the department was still not a completely happy one. Wright had kept power and the control of the research funds very largely in his own hands.

He was now an elderly man. Both of his most likely successors, Fleming and Freeman, were themselves nearing retirement age. Over the years they had been played off against one another, with each being promised that he eventually would take control.

Ultimately, the announcement of Fleming's knighthood settled the issue. On that day, there was tea as usual in the library. Very few of the old staff were still around—only those who had been called in to help with the clinics, teaching, or vaccine production. They joined Wright at tea. He was unusually silent. Fleming came in and sat down. Not a word was said. The secretary came in with a bundle of papers, mainly to do with the vaccine business, and held them out to Wright. He waved them away, saying, "Dr. Fleming will deal with them. They are too unimportant for me."

Fleming had by then been a professor for twenty years and his knighthood had been announced in *The Times* that day. This was the Old Man's last gesture as power finally slipped from him, after more than forty years of absolute supremacy over his department. Fleming took the papers and went out, still without saying anything.

THE FLEMING MYTH

"Alec Fleming was an exceedingly shy man," noted his former St. Mary's colleague and biographer W. Howard Hughes. "He deliberately hid the truth about himself. When he was famous, all press cuttings about him were sent to his secretary. All the false stories invented by journalists and others were collected in a special file to make up what we called the 'Fleming Myth.' He would tell all these stories at dinner parties with a perfectly straight face. The more unlikely they were, the more they appealed to him. They let the real man hide away, and this is what he seemed to want."

Fleming was now sixty-three years old—very near the age of retirement for professors. It was natural that he should become director of the department, which was renamed the Wright-Fleming Institute. A new full-time professor and staff were appointed as soon as men were released from the armed forces and the Emergency Medical Service. These people would deal with all the routine jobs that Fleming hated, while Fleming would be able to concentrate the rest of his time on teaching postgraduates, directing the institute's research, and conducting his own research work.

With the end of the war in Europe in May 1945, the London hospitals reopened fully. The British government's Medical Research Council established a unit to study the effects of new antibiotics on sick patients. Just as salvarsan had once been sent to Wright for trial, now new antibiotics were sent to Fleming, to test whether they could be used for treating tuberculosis. Thankfully, the tragedies of Wright's days did not recur—none of the workers died—but still, far too many lab workers developed tuberculosis during the trials. There were, for example, no protective cabinets to work in. The cultures of tubercle bacilli were tested in test tubes on the open bench. Almost everyone working there had to go, at some time or another, to a sanatorium for treatment. Under Fleming's direction, many safety precautions were implemented that would become standard in modern research laboratories.

The 1940s and 1950s was a time of triumph for Fleming, and he was invited to many countries as a hero. Yet he was still a very poor public speaker, and people who went to listen to him were usually disappointed. He was happiest during his visits to the United States and to Spain. His deadpan delivery and short, witty replies to newspaper men were well received in the United States. When he was in Spain, he delivered his speeches in English; when translated, they sounded much less flat.

For some reason the Spanish seemed quicker to honor him, and were more generous toward him, than any other people. Fleming collected honorary degrees, and the silk hoods that went with them, from many places but it was a Spanish hood that he wore on most ceremonial occasions. This, he joked, was because they gave him both a hood and the gown to go with it!

The Nobel Prize was not the only important award that Fleming received. Over the next ten years, Fleming received many other awards, some of them very valuable and beautiful works of art. He never bragged about them or showed off to his colleagues. The only hospital people to see his awards were some of the technicians who worked with him, as well as a carpenter in the university's workshop who made a cabinet to hold them.

Fleming found receiving awards to be very embarrassing. He thought up a way of getting over this uneasiness. He grew his mold on black paper, so it could be lifted off the culture medium when growth was complete. The paper discs, about an inch across, were then fixed and dried. They fitted neatly into little glass frames with tortoiseshell backs and a space where he could write something

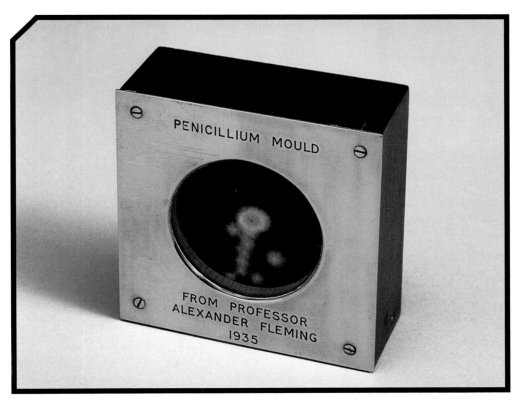

A sample of penicillium mold that Fleming gave to a neighbor in an ornamental case.

Alexander Fleming was revered in Spain. This statue in Madrid depicts a matador saluting Fleming with his montera, the hat worn in the arena. An inscription reads, "To Dr Fleming with the gratitude of bullfighters."

suitable for the occasion. His brother Robert, who worked in the optical industry, made special frames for him. One of them came in handy when he went to receive the medal of the Papal Academy of Science from the Pope. When the Pope awarded the medal, Fleming in return gave him one of the framed discs of antibiotic mold.

Final Years

These months of recognition should have been very happy for Fleming, but they were spoiled by the tragic illness of his wife, Sarah. She had an incurable disease of the spine. They went together to Spain but she became even more seriously ill there, and had to stay in the hotel in Madrid, unable to go with him to the special meeting that had been arranged at the universities in Madrid and elsewhere. She came back to England to face a final illness, and died in 1949.

During this last illness, Fleming was desolate. He would sit looking into space, doing and saying nothing. Luckily some of his staff was around to give him the only treatment likely to help. They would set up experiments and take the results to him for checking and interpreting. The subject for study was the change brought about in bacteria by penicillin and other drugs. One effect of penicillin was to make the bacteria swell up and burst. Somehow it stopped them building strong cell walls, but did not stop them growing. Soon he was so interested that he returned to work again.

Before the first results were published, another fortunate thing happened. As had happened with vaccines in Wright's time, foreign workers now came to the department to learn the latest methods and find out about antibiotics. One of them was Amalia Koutsouri-Vourekas, a Greek doctor who had suffered as

Lady Amalia Fleming unveils a bust of her husband in 1956.

a prisoner in a German concentration camp. She came as much to relax and regain her strength, as to study and learn. Fleming allowed her to join the team, as the other scientists were heavily committed to the hospital work and had little time for research. After a while, she was sufficiently trained for Fleming to take her on as his research assistant.

Amalia spoke four or five European languages and so was particularly helpful in showing foreign visitors around and interpreting for them. Later, after Lady Fleming's death, she acted as Fleming's hostess and took from him the strain of entertaining his guests. He missed her very much when her scholarship ended and she had to return to Athens. And it came as no surprise to those who worked with Fleming that he stopped in Athens on his way back from a tour of India, and later announced that she would be the second Lady Fleming. The marriage lasted a happy two years. In March 1955, just after he retired from the institute, Alexander Fleming died of a heart attack.

When Fleming died, tributes to him poured in. Eloquent obituary notices appeared in newspapers and medical journals throughout the world. "Fleming," noted one in the *British Medical Journal*, "had the real naturalist's capacity for observation and the scientific imagination to see the implications of the observed fact."

There were many simpler expressions of respect, such as that shown by flower-sellers in Barcelona who emptied their baskets in front of a tablet commemorating his visit to their city. Indeed, the shy and reserved Fleming would have appreciated such tributes as these more than all the speeches and essays of his colleagues throughout the world, just as of all the monuments erected to his memory he would have most liked the one set up at his birthplace, Lochfield farm in Ayrshire, Scotland, which bore the simple inscription:

ALEXANDER FLEMING

discoverer of penicillin
was born here at Lochfield
on 6th August 1881

TEXT-DEPENDENT QUESTIONS

1. Who was the first civilian patient whose life was saved by penicillin treatment?

2. In what year did Fleming receive the Nobel Prize for Medicine?

3. Who did Fleming marry in 1953?

 # RESEARCH PROJECT

The United Nations, or U.N., formed in 1945 with the goal of preventing another world war. Ambassadors from around the world meet to discuss international problems, and U.N. agencies have helped to curb the spread of disease in poor, developing countries by providing antibiotics and other useful medicines. Research the U.N. to find out why some people praise it and others criticize it. Write a one-page paper describing your own opinion about the U.N.

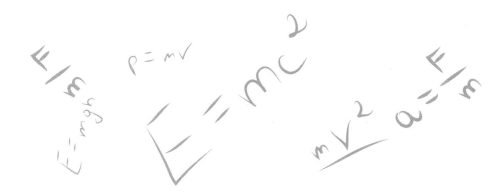

Chronology

1683

Antoni van Leeuwenhoek first sees and describes bacteria using a microscope.

1835–36

Agostino Bassi shows that the silkworm disease muscardine is caused by a tiny fungus.

1866

Louis Pasteur shows that another silkworm disease, *pébrine*, is caused by a living organism.

1877

Pasteur proves that anthrax is caused by a bacillus that was first noticed by German bacteriologist Aloys Pollender in 1849.

1880

Pasteur succeeds in attenuating, or weakening, an anthrax culture for use in vaccination.

1881

Alexander Fleming is born on August 6.

1884

Elie Metchnikoff shows that white blood cells are able to surround and destroy invading germs.

1895

Fleming arrives in London and starts work as an office clerk.

1896

Almroth Wright announces the discovery of his typhoid vaccine.

1897
Fleming attends the Polytechnic School on Regent Street, London.

1899–1902
The Boer War in South Africa.

1900
Fleming joins the London Scottish Regiment.

1901
Fleming's legacy and scholarship enable him to study medicine at St. Mary's.

1902
Wright is appointed as a professor at St. Mary's.

1906
Fleming joins Wright's department.

1908
Fleming passes his final medical examinations, winning the gold medal of the University of London. He also becomes a fellow of the Royal College of Surgeons.

1909
Paul Ehrlich shows that "606" (salvarsan), one of the first successful modern chemotherapeutic agents, is active against the germs that cause syphilis.

1911
Fleming uses Ehrlich's salvarsan successfully in the treatment of syphilis.

1914
The First World War begins. Fleming serves in France at the 13th General Hospital in Boulogne.

1915
Fleming marries Sarah McElroy on December 23.

1918
The First World War ends. Fleming returns to St. Mary's, where he works as a lecturer.

1920
Fleming is appointed director of the Department of Systematic Bacteriology and assistant director of the Inoculation Department at St. Mary's.

1922
Fleming discovers lysozyme.

1928
Fleming becomes a professor at St. Mary's.

1929
Fleming discovers penicillin.

1936
Leonard Colebrook at Queen Charlotte's Hospital announces the successful use of sulfanilamide.

1939
The Second World War begins. Fleming appointed sector pathologist at Harefield.

1940
Howard Florey and Ernst Chain publish the results of their work on penicillin.

1941
First human patient treated with penicillin.

1944
Fleming is knighted.

1945
The Second World War ends. Fleming, Florey, and Chain win the Nobel Prize for Medicine.

1946
Fleming becomes director of the newly renamed Wright-Fleming Institute.

1949
Sarah Fleming dies.

1953
Fleming marries Amalia Voureka on April 9.

1955
Fleming dies on March 11.

Further Reading

Brown, Kevin. *Penicillin Man: Alexander Fleming and the Antibiotic Revolution.* New York: The History Press, 2005.

Chapman, Allan. *Physicians, Plagues, and Progress: The History of Western Medicine from Antiquity to Antibiotics.* Oxford, UK: Lion Books, 2016.

Gallagher, Jason C., and Conan MacDougall. *Antibiotics Simplified.* 4th Ed. Burlington, Mass.: Jones & Bartlett Learning, 2018.

Jong-Kang Liu and King-Thom Chung. *Pioneers in Microbiology: The Human Side of Science.* Hackensack, N.J.: World Scientific, 2018.

Lax, Eric. *The Mold in Dr. Florey's Coat: The Story of the Penicillin Miracle.* New York: Henry Holt and Co., 2015.

Morus, Iwan Rhys. *The Oxford Illustrated History of Science.* New York: Oxford University Press, 2017.

Rosen, William. *Miracle Cure: The Creation of Antibiotics and the Birth of Modern Medicine.* New York: Viking, 2017.

Wootton, David. *The Invention of Science: A New History of the Scientific Revolution.* New York: Harper Perennial, 2016.

Zamosky, Lisa. *Louis Pasteur and the Fight Against Germs.* Huntington Beach, Calif.: Teacher Created Materials, 2008.

Internet Resources

www.ncbi.nlm.nih.gov/pmc/articles/PMC4520913

Biographical information about Alexander Fleming is available at this site managed by the National Center for Biotechnology Information, which advances science and health by providing access to biomedical and genomic information. It is part of the National Institutes of Health, an agency of the U.S. Department of Health and Human Services.

www.bbc.co.uk/history/historic_figures/fleming_alexander.shtml

The British Broadcasting Company (BBC) provides a short biography of Alexander Fleming at this site.

https://www.asm.org

The American Society for Microbiology is the world's oldest and largest life science organization. The official ASM website contains links to articles and exhibits related to microbiology.

http://www.pbs.org/wgbh/nova

The website of *NOVA*, a science series that airs on PBS. The series produces in-depth science programming on a variety of topics, from the latest breakthroughs in technology to the deepest mysteries of the natural world.

http://www.biology4kids.com/files/studies_scimethod.html

A simple explanation of the scientific method is available at this website for young people.

Series Glossary of Key Terms

anomaly—something that differs from the expectations generated by an established scientific idea. Anomalous observations may inspire scientists to reconsider, modify, or come up with alternatives to an accepted theory or hypothesis.

evidence—test results and/or observations that may either help support or help refute a scientific idea. In general, raw data are considered evidence only once they have been interpreted in a way that reflects on the accuracy of a scientific idea.

experiment—a scientific test that involves manipulating some factor or factors in a system in order to see how those changes affect the outcome or behavior of the system.

hypothesis—a proposed explanation for a fairly narrow set of phenomena, usually based on prior experience, scientific background knowledge, preliminary observations, and logic.

natural world—all the components of the physical universe, as well as the natural forces at work on those things.

objective—to consider and represent facts without being influenced by biases, opinions, or emotions. Scientists strive to be objective, not subjective, in their reasoning about scientific issues.

observe—to note, record, or attend to a result, occurrence, or phenomenon.

science—knowledge of the natural world, as well as the process through which that knowledge is built through testing ideas with evidence gathered from the natural world.

subjective—referring to something that is influenced by biases, opinions, and/or emotions. Scientists strive to be objective, not subjective, in their reasoning about scientific issues.

test—an observation or experiment that could provide evidence regarding the accuracy of a scientific idea. Testing involves figuring out what one would expect to observe if an idea were correct and comparing that expectation to what one actually observes.

theory—a broad, natural explanation for a wide range of phenomena in science. Theories are concise, coherent, systematic, predictive, and broadly applicable, often integrating and generalizing many hypotheses. Theories accepted by the scientific community are generally strongly supported by many different lines of evidence. However, theories may be modified or overturned as new evidence is discovered.

Index

A

advertisment (illustration), 72–73
allergist, 18, 19, 37
Allison, V.D., 42–43
ampoules, 38, 70
anilines (dye), 29
anthrax (disease), 23, 25
antibiotic, 32, 39, 66, 67 (QR code), 76
antiseptic chemicals, 35–37, 40, 48, 51
Antwerp (Belgium), 36
Arsphenamine (vaccine), 41
Aryshire (Scotland), 6
asepsis, 32, 37
attenuate, 18, 23, 25

B

bacillus, 18, 23, 25, 61
bacteria, discovery of, 23, 27
bactericidal, 32, 44
bacteriology, 18, 19, 21, 27, 30, 39, 64
Bacteriology Department (St.Mary's), 12, 18, 19
Balfour (Lord), 14
Bassi, Agostino, 23
battlefield medicine (WWI), 37 (QR code), 63, 72
biochemist, role in bacteriology, 64–65
biochemistry, study of, 59
bleach (hypochlorite solution), 36
blood protein, 59–60
Boer War (1900), 9, 10–11, 18, 19, 32
Boulogne (France), 32, 33, 35
British Journal of Experimental Pathology (1929), 54, 55
British Medical Journal, 82

C

Cambridge University, 65
Casino (13th General Hospital), 33, 35, 36
Chain, Ernst, 64, 65, 66, 67–69, 75
Chelsea Art Club, 50
chemotherapeutic agents, 28
chemotherapy, 58, 63
childbed fever, 21
cholera, 72

Colebrook, Leonard, 19, 21, 33, 35, 39, 63, 64, 74
colony, 46, 47, 51
Craddock, Stuart, 60

D

Daraine, Casimir Joseph, 23
Darvel (Scotland), 7
diptheria bacillus, 61, 72
disease, treatment of, 28
Douglas, Stewart Ranken, 19, 33, 37
dust asthma, 52
Duthie, 65
dye, 29, 63
dysentery, 38

E

Edinburgh University Solution (Eusol), 36
Ehrlich, Paul, 28, 30, 41
Emergency Medical Service (London), 75, 78
enzyme, 32, 42
Eusol (Edinburgh University Solution), 36

F

farm life, 6, 7, 8
fermentation vessel, 68, 76
Fleming, Alexander (Alec)
    birth, family history and death, 6, 7, 8–9, 82
    character, 12, 16, 40, 48, 50, 55, 62, 77
    education, 9, 11–12
    interests, 7, 9, 11, 61
    medical career, 30, 35, 39, 40, 41, 42–43, 60–62
    pathologist, role of, 72
    portraits, 57, 61, 80
    quotes, 9, 35, 44, 49, 60
    research, value of, 43–44, 62, 68
    sports, 7, 9, 11
Fleming, Grace (mother), 7
Fleming, Hugh (brother), 8
Fleming, John (brother), 8, 9
Fleming, John (uncle), 9
Fleming, Robert (brother), 8, 9, 80
Fleming, Sarah (wife), 80–81
Fleming, Tom (brother), 8
Florey, Howard Walter, 64, 65–67, 71, 75
fowl cholera (disease), 23, 25
Fredericq, P., 66

Freeman, John, 11, 14, 19, 21, 33, 37, 52
fungus ergot, 69

G
germ theory of disease, 24, 26, 51, 75
germs (microbes), 23, 61
globulin, 58, 60
Gratia, André, 66
Great Britian, 71
Guiness, Arthur, 14

H
H Company (Territorial Army), 9
hayfever, 19, 21, 39, 52
Hoffman, Erich, 28
honours, 6, 11
Hopkins, Gowland, 65
Hughes, W. Howard, 50, 62, 77
hypochlorite solution (bleach), 36

I
immunology, 18, 28, 59
infection, treatment of, 59
inflammation, of the body, 65
influenza, 53, 72

J
Jenner, Edward, 68

K
Kilmarnock (Scotland), 7, 8
kirk, 6, 7
knighthood, 77
Koch, Robert, 27
Koutsouri-Vourekas, Amalia (second wife), 81, 82

L
La Touche, Charles J., 52, 55
Lancet (medical journal), 67
Life magazine, 72–73
Lister, Joseph, 21, 25, 26, 35, 39, 68
London School of Tropical Medicine and Hygiene, 60
London Scottish (Territorial Army), 9, 10–11, 19
London, England, 8
Loudoun Moor, 7, 8
lysis (cell destruction), 51

lysozyme (human), 42, 43–44, 47, 51, 60, 65

M
malaria, 28, 44
marksmanship, 9, 11
Maurois, André, 33
Medical Research Club, 55
Medical Research Council (British), 78
Medical Research Council (laboratory), 37
medical research, funding of, 12
mercury, 28
Metchnikoff, Elie, 27, 29, 43
microbes (germs), 23, 61
microscope, 22, 23, 29, 68
Minister of Supply, 71
mold spores, 46, 48, 49, 52, 55, 60
muscardine (disease), 23
mycologist, 46, 52

N
naturalist, Victorian, 68
Nazi Germany, 71
neosalvarsan, 40
nicknames, 50
Nobel Prize for Medicine, 30, 65, 75–76, 79
Noon, Leonard, 19, 20, 21

O
obituary, 82
On the Antibacterial Action of Cultures of a Penicillim, 55–56
Oxford University, 64, 66, 67

P
Papal Academy of Science, 80
Parke Davis (U.S.), 39
Pasteur, Louis, 23, 24, 25, 27, 39, 68
patent, 70, 74
patent medicine, 74
pathologist, role of, 72, 75
pébrine (disease), 23
penicillin
    bacteria, role of, 51 (QR code)
    documentation of, 53, 54
    large-scale production of, 71–72, 75 (QR code), 76, 92
    mold spores, 46, 48, 49

preparation of, 60
re-emergence of, 64–65
Penicillin as a Chemotherapeutic Agent, 67
Penicillium, 48, 55, 58, 59, 68, 71, 79
phagocytosis, 32, 44
pike eggs, 43
Pollender, Franz Aloys, 23
Polytechnic School (London), 8–9
potency, 58, 59
powder, 65, 67
prontosil (dye), 63
Pryce, Merlin, 48
Public Health Laboratory Service (London), 75
public school, 6, 12
puerperal fever, 63

Q
Queen Charlotte's Hospital, 21, 39, 63
quinine, 28, 44

R
Raistrick, Harold, 60
Red Cross Organization, 72
research team, St.Mary's, 19
resistance (penicillin), 61
Ridley, Frederick, 60
Royal Army Medical Corps, 20, 34–35
Royal College of Surgeons, 11
Royal Society of Medicine, 43
Royal Victoria Military Hospital (Netley), 18
rye (disease), 69

S
salvarsan ("606"), 29, 40, 41
Savage Club, 50
Schaudinn, Fritz, 28
Scottish War for Independence, 8
Second World War (WWII), 55, 70, 71
sensitivity (penicillin), 61
Shaw, George Bernard, 14
Silences of Colonel Bramble, 33, 35
Spanish (language), 78

Spanish Civil War, 72
Spilsbury, Bernard, 19
spore cultures, 52
St.Mary's Hospital (Paddington), 9, 11, 12–13, 16
    (QR code), 18, 20, 37, 49, 60, 71
staphylococcus, 46, 47–48, 49, 51, 61
streptococcus, 58, 63, 64, 67
suphanilamide, 64, 74
syphilis, 18, 28, 30, 41

T
teamwork, medical school, 14, 16, 33, 35, 37, 52
temperature, role of, 53, 55
Territorial Army (London Scottish), 9, 10–11, 19
tetanus, 32, 33, 72
Times (newspaper), 67, 77
toxin, 70
toxoid, 70
Trefouel, Jacques, 66
Treponema pallidum (bacteria), 28–29
tuberculosis, 20, 78
typhoid, vaccine, 18, 20, 33, 72

U
University of London, 9, 11, 60

V
vaccine, 18, 23, 25 (QR code), 27, 38, 72
van Leeuwenhoek, Antonie, 22, 23

W
Waksman, Selman, 66
water polo, 9, 11
Wells, John Herbert, 20
Welsch, Maurice, 66
white blood cells (disease), 27, 29, 64
whooping cough, 72
Wright-Fleming Institute, 78
Wright, Almroth ("Old Man"), 11, 12, 14, 15, 18,
    20, 28, 30, 32, 36, 76–77
WWII (Second World War), 55, 70, 71

About the Author

Bradley Sneddon is a graduate of the University of Delaware. He teaches biology in Newark, Delaware, where he lives with his wife and their two dogs. He has also written biographies of Benjamin Franklin and Charles Darwin for Mason Crest's SCIENTISTS AND THEIR DISCOVERIES series.

Photo Credits